whoopie pies

METRO BOOKS
New York

6ft
3JT
425

Contents

Introduction

Everybody loves cake. Everybody loves cookies. So who wouldn't love whoopie pies?

These sandwiched cakey-cookies, which are taking the world by storm, originated in either Pennsylvania or Maine (depending on who you believe), where they were packed into the lunch boxes of Amish farmers. *Whoopie Pies* takes this traditional favorite, pays homage to it, and then has some fun.

Within these pages you will find 55 fabulous whoopies, all with their own unique character. The flavors range from traditional, such as pumpkin or classic chocolate with a marshmallow filling, to contemporary, featuring green tea and cherry or sweet polenta and rosemary. Whether you're 1 or 100, you'll find a whoopie (or 20) to tempt your tastebuds. Take your pick from playful, fun, and kid-friendly whoopies such as banana splits or doughnuts, or whoopies dedicated to the finer things—grownup whoopies such as espresso or raspberry cheesecake.

At the back of this book you'll find a handy section of basics that will provide the fillings you need to bring your whoopies to life. Feel free to create your own personalized whoopies, combining your favorite whoopie halves and your choice of filling.

If you haven't discovered whoopies yet, now is the time to find out what the craze is all about. It's whoopie time!

Classic
flavors

Classic chocolate whoopies

Preparation time: 20 minutes
Cooking time: 12 minutes
Makes: 14

1 stick unsalted butter, just softened
½ cup (firmly packed) soft brown sugar
1 egg, at room temperature
1 teaspoon vanilla extract
1 cup all-purpose flour
¼ cup unsweetened cocoa powder
1 teaspoon baking powder
½ teaspoon baking soda
⅓ cup buttermilk
1 quantity marshmallow frosting (see page 123)

TIP: Keep unfilled whoopies in an airtight container at room temperature for up to 2 days. They are best filled just before serving.

1 Preheat the oven to 350°F. Line three large baking sheets with baking paper.

2 Use an electric mixer to beat the butter and sugar in a medium bowl, scraping down the side as necessary, until pale and creamy. Add the egg and vanilla and beat well.

3 Sift the flour, cocoa, baking powder, and baking soda together. With the mixer on low speed, add the flour mixture and buttermilk alternately in two separate batches each. Beat on low speed for 2 minutes or until well combined.

4 Use a ¾ inch plain nozzle to pipe 28 x 2 inch rounds of the mixture onto the baking sheets, leaving 2 inches between them to allow for spreading. Bake for 12 minutes, swapping the sheets around after 8 minutes, or until just firm to the touch. Allow to cool for 2 minutes on the baking sheets then transfer to a cake rack to cool completely.

5 Spread the marshmallow frosting over the flat sides of half the whoopies. Sandwich with the remaining whoopies.

Choc-orange whoopies

Preparation time: 30 minutes
Cooking time: 10 minutes
Makes: 18

1 stick unsalted butter, just softened
⅔ cup (firmly packed) soft brown sugar
1 egg, at room temperature
1 teaspoon vanilla extract
1½ cups all-purpose flour
⅔ cup unsweetened cocoa powder, plus extra, to dust
1 teaspoon baking powder
½ teaspoon baking soda
¾ cup milk
1 quantity vanilla buttercream (see page 118), made
   with 2 teaspoons finely grated orange zest
½ cup orange-coated chocolate balls, coarsely chopped

TIP: Keep filled whoopies in an airtight container in the fridge for up to 3 days. Serve at room temperature.

1 Preheat the oven to 350°F. Line three large baking sheets with baking paper.
2 Use an electric mixer to beat the butter and sugar in a medium bowl, scraping down the side as necessary, until pale and creamy. Add the egg and vanilla and beat well.
3 Sift the flour, cocoa, baking powder, and baking soda together. With the mixer on low speed, add the flour mixture and milk alternately in two separate batches each. Beat on low speed until just combined.
4 Spoon 36 even tablespoonfuls of the mixture onto the baking sheets, leaving 2 inches between them to allow for spreading. Bake for 8–10 minutes, swapping the baking sheets around after 6 minutes. The whoopies will still be a little soft to the touch. (Do not overcook, otherwise they will dry out.) Allow to cool for 2 minutes on the baking sheets then transfer to a cake rack to cool completely.
5 Spread the buttercream onto the flat sides of half the whoopies, spreading to the edges. Sandwich with the remaining whoopies. Roll the sides of the whoopies in the chopped orange-coated chocolate balls to coat. Dust with extra cocoa powder.

Strawberries & cream whoopies

Preparation time: 25 minutes
Cooking time: 12 minutes
Makes: 16

1 stick unsalted butter, just softened
½ cup superfine sugar
1 egg, at room temperature
2 teaspoons vanilla extract
1½ cups all-purpose flour
½ teaspoon baking powder
1 teaspoon baking soda
⅓ cup buttermilk
1¼ cups whipping cream
1 teaspoon vanilla bean paste or 1 vanilla bean,
   halved lengthwise, seeds scraped
⅓ cup strawberry jam
1¼ cups thinly sliced strawberries
confectioners' sugar, to dust

> **TIP:** Keep unfilled whoopies in an airtight container at room temperature for up to 2 days. They are best filled just before serving.

1 Preheat the oven to 350°F. Line three large baking sheets with baking paper.

2 Use an electric mixer to beat the butter and sugar in a medium bowl, scraping down the side as necessary, until pale and creamy. Add the egg and vanilla and beat well.

3 Sift the flour, baking powder, and baking soda together. With the mixer on low speed, add the flour mixture and buttermilk alternately in two separate batches each. Beat on low speed for 2 minutes or until well combined.

4 Use a ¾ inch plain nozzle to pipe 32 x 1½ inch rounds of the mixture onto the baking sheets, leaving 2 inches between them to allow for spreading. Bake for 10–12 minutes, swapping the baking sheets around halfway through cooking, or until light golden and just firm to the touch. Allow to cool for 2 minutes on the baking sheets then transfer to a cake rack to cool completely.

5 Use an electric mixer to whisk the cream and vanilla in a small bowl until firm peaks form. Spread the flat sides of half the whoopies with the jam. Top with the strawberries. Spread the flat sides of the remaining whoopies with the cream, then sandwich with the strawberry whoopies. Dust with confectioners' sugar.

Hermit whoopies

Preparation time: 40 minutes
Cooking time: 12 minutes
Makes: 30

1 stick unsalted butter, just softened
¾ cup (firmly packed) soft brown sugar
1 egg, at room temperature
1½ teaspoons vanilla extract
2 cups all-purpose flour
1 teaspoon baking powder
½ teaspoon baking soda
3 teaspoons mixed spice
½ cup buttermilk
1 cup pecans, finely chopped
1 cup raisins, chopped
1 quantity vanilla buttercream (see page 118),
   made with 2 tablespoons molasses
confectioners' sugar, to dust

TIP: Keep filled whoopies in an airtight container in the fridge for up to 3 days. Serve at room temperature.

1 Preheat the oven to 350°F. Line three large baking sheets with baking paper.
2 Use an electric mixer to beat the butter and sugar in a medium bowl, scraping down the side as necessary, until pale and creamy. Add the egg and vanilla and beat well.
3 Sift the flour, baking powder, baking soda, and mixed spice together. With the mixer on low speed, add the flour mixture and buttermilk alternately in two separate batches each. Beat on low speed for 2 minutes or until well combined. Add the pecans and raisins and stir to combine well.

4 Spoon 60 even, heaping teaspoonfuls of the mixture onto the baking sheets, leaving 2 inches between them to allow for spreading. Bake for 12 minutes, swapping the baking sheets around after 8 minutes, or until firm to the touch. Allow to cool for 2 minutes on the baking sheets then transfer to a cake rack to cool completely.
5 Spread or use a ½ inch star nozzle to pipe the buttercream onto the flat sides of half the whoopies. Sandwich with the remaining whoopies. Dust with confectioners' sugar.

Pumpkin whoopies

Preparation time: 25 minutes
Cooking time: 12 minutes
Makes: 12

1 stick unsalted butter, just softened
1 cup (firmly packed) soft brown sugar
1 egg, at room temperature
1 teaspoon vanilla extract
1 cup puréed cooked pumpkin
2 cups all-purpose flour
1½ teaspoons baking powder
½ teaspoon baking soda
2 teaspoons ground cinnamon
1 teaspoon ground nutmeg
1 quantity cream cheese frosting (see page 121)
confectioners' sugar, to dust

TIP: Keep filled whoopies in an airtight container in the fridge for up to 3 days. Serve at room temperature.

1 Preheat the oven to 350°F. Line three large baking sheets with baking paper.
2 Use an electric mixer to beat the butter and sugar in a medium bowl, scraping down the side as necessary, until pale and creamy. Add the egg, vanilla, and pumpkin. Beat on low speed until just combined.
3 Sift the flour, baking powder, baking soda, cinnamon, and nutmeg together and add to the butter mixture. Beat on low speed until just combined.
4 Spoon 24 heaping tablespoonfuls of the mixture onto the baking sheets, leaving 2 inches between them to allow for spreading. Bake for 10–12 minutes, swapping the baking sheets around after 8 minutes, or until just firm to the touch. Allow to cool for 2 minutes on the baking sheets then transfer to a cake rack to cool completely.
5 Spread the cream cheese frosting onto the flat sides of half the whoopies. Sandwich with the remaining whoopies. Dust with confectioners' sugar.

Gingerbread whoopies

Preparation time: 20 minutes (+ 30 minutes chilling time)
Cooking time: 12 minutes
Makes: 16

1 stick unsalted butter, just softened
½ cup (firmly packed) soft brown sugar
¼ cup light treacle or maple syrup
1 egg, at room temperature
1 teaspoon vanilla extract
1½ cups all-purpose flour
3 teaspoons ground ginger
1 teaspoon mixed spice
1 teaspoon baking powder
1 teaspoon baking soda
⅔ cup buttermilk

Maple syrup frosting
6 ounces cream cheese, just softened
½ stick unsalted butter, just softened
2 cups confectioners' sugar, sifted
¼ cup maple syrup or light treacle

TIP: Keep filled whoopies in an airtight container in the fridge for up to 3 days. Serve at room temperature.

1 Preheat the oven to 350°F. Line three large baking sheets with baking paper.
2 Use an electric mixer to beat the butter, sugar, and treacle or syrup in a medium bowl, scraping down the side as necessary, until pale and creamy. Add egg and vanilla and beat well.
3 Sift the flour, spices, baking powder, and baking soda together. With the mixer on low speed, add the flour mixture and buttermilk alternately in two separate batches each. Beat on low speed for 2 minutes or until well combined.
4 Use a ¾ inch plain nozzle to pipe 32 x 1¾ inch rounds of the mixture onto the baking sheets, leaving 2 inches between them to allow for spreading. Bake for 12 minutes, swapping the baking sheets around halfway through cooking, or until light golden and just firm to the touch. Cool for 2 minutes on the sheets then transfer to a cake rack to cool completely.
5 For the frosting, use an electric mixer to beat the cream cheese and butter until well combined. Beat in the confectioners' sugar, ½ cup at a time, until well combined. Beat in the maple syrup. Cover and refrigerate for 30 minutes or until firm.
6 Use a ½ inch plain nozzle to pipe the frosting onto the flat sides of half the whoopies. Sandwich with the remaining whoopies.

Coconut whoopies

Preparation time: 30 minutes
Cooking time: 12 minutes
Makes: 14

⅓ cup unsalted butter, just softened
⅓ cup superfine sugar
1 egg, at room temperature
1 teaspoon vanilla extract
1 cup all-purpose flour
1 teaspoon baking powder
½ teaspoon baking soda
¼ cup milk
⅔ cup shredded coconut
½ quantity marshmallow frosting (see page 123),
   made with 1 teaspoon coconut extract, or to taste
½ cup shredded coconut, extra, lightly toasted,
   to decorate

TIP: Keep unfilled whoopies in an airtight container at room temperature for up to 2 days. They are best filled just before serving.

1 Preheat the oven to 350°F. Line three large baking sheets with baking paper.
2 Use an electric mixer to beat the butter and sugar in a medium bowl, scraping down the side as necessary, until pale and creamy. Add the egg and vanilla and beat well.
3 Sift the flour, baking powder, and baking soda together. With the mixer on low speed, add the flour mixture and milk alternately in two separate batches each. Beat on low speed for 2 minutes or until well combined. Fold through the coconut.

4 Use a ¾ inch plain nozzle to pipe 28 x 1½ inch rounds of the mixture onto the baking sheets, leaving 2 inches between them to allow for spreading. Bake for 10–12 minutes, swapping the baking sheets around after 8 minutes, or until light golden and just firm to the touch. Allow to cool for 2 minutes on the baking sheets then transfer to a cake rack to cool completely.
5 Use a ½ inch plain nozzle to pipe the warm marshmallow frosting onto the flat sides of half the whoopies, spreading to the edges. Sandwich with the remaining whoopies. Roll the sides of the whoopies in the extra coconut to coat.

Vanilla whoopies

Preparation time: 25 minutes
Cooking time: 12 minutes
Makes: 14

1 stick unsalted butter, just softened
¾ cup superfine sugar
1 egg, at room temperature
1 teaspoon vanilla extract
2 cups all-purpose flour
1 teaspoon baking powder
½ teaspoon bicarbonate of soda
⅔ cup milk
⅔ quantity marshmallow frosting (see page 123)
confectioners' sugar, to dust

TIP: Keep unfilled whoopies in an airtight container at room temperature for up to 2 days. They are best filled just before serving.

1 Preheat the oven to 350°F. Line three large baking sheets with baking paper.
2 Use an electric mixer to beat the butter and sugar in a medium bowl, scraping down the side as necessary, until pale and creamy. Add the egg and vanilla and beat well.
3 Sift the flour, baking powder, and baking soda together. With the mixer on low speed, add the flour mixture and milk alternately in two separate batches each. Beat on low speed for 2 minutes or until well combined.
4 Pipe or spoon 28 even, heaping tablespoonfuls of the mixture onto the baking sheets, leaving 2 inches between them to allow for spreading. Bake for 10–12 minutes, swapping the baking sheets around after 8 minutes, or until light golden and just firm to the touch. Allow to cool for 2 minutes on the baking sheets then transfer to a cake rack to cool completely.
5 Spread or use a ¾ inch plain nozzle to pipe the warm marshmallow frosting onto the flat sides of half the whoopies. Sandwich with the remaining whoopies. Dust with confectioners' sugar.

S'mores whoopies

Preparation time: 25 minutes
Cooking time: 12 minutes
Makes: 12

1 stick unsalted butter, just softened
¾ cup (firmly packed) soft brown sugar
1 egg, at room temperature
1½ teaspoons vanilla extract
2 cups all-purpose whole-wheat flour
1 teaspoon baking powder
½ teaspoon baking soda
½ cup milk
⅔ quantity dark chocolate ganache
(see page 122)
⅓ quantity marshmallow frosting (see page 123),
made with pink marshmallows

> **TIP:** Keep unfilled whoopies in an airtight container at room temperature for up to 2 days. They are best filled just before serving.

1 Preheat the oven to 350°F. Line three large baking sheets with baking paper.
2 Use an electric mixer to beat the butter and sugar in a medium bowl, scraping down the side as necessary, until pale and creamy. Add the egg and vanilla and beat well.
3 Sift the flour, baking powder, and baking soda together, returning the flour solids to the mixture. With the mixer on low speed, add the flour mixture and milk alternately in two separate batches each. Beat on low speed for 2 minutes or until well combined.
4 Use a ¾ inch plain nozzle to pipe 24 x 2¼ inch rounds of the mixture onto the baking sheets, leaving 2 inches between them to allow for spreading. Bake for 12 minutes, swapping the baking sheets around halfway through cooking, or until light golden and firm to the touch. Allow to cool for 2 minutes on the baking sheets then transfer to a cake rack to cool completely.
5 Spread the flat sides of half the whoopies with the chocolate ganache. Spread the remaining whoopies with the warm marshmallow frosting. Allow to stand until the frosting is firm but not set. Sandwich the ganache-covered whoopies with the marshmallow-covered whoopies, gently pressing together.

Carrot cake whoopies
with cream cheese frosting

Preparation time: 25 minutes
Cooking time: 12 minutes
Makes: 12

1 stick unsalted butter, just softened
1 cup (firmly packed) dark brown sugar
1 egg, at room temperature
1 teaspoon vanilla extract
⅔ cup (firmly packed) coarsely shredded carrot
2 cups all-purpose flour
2 teaspoons baking powder
½ teaspoon baking soda
2 teaspoons ground cinnamon
2 teaspoons ground nutmeg
⅔ cup buttermilk
½ cup walnuts, chopped
1 quantity cream cheese frosting (see page 121), made
   with 1 tablespoon finely grated lemon zest
½ cup walnuts, extra, chopped
12 walnut halves, to decorate

TIP: Keep filled whoopies in an airtight container in the fridge for up to 3 days. Serve at room temperature.

1 Preheat the oven to 350°F. Line three large baking sheets with baking paper.
2 Use an electric mixer to beat the butter and sugar in a medium bowl, scraping down the side as necessary, until pale and creamy. Add the egg, vanilla, and carrot and beat well.
3 Sift the flour, baking powder, baking soda, cinnamon, and nutmeg together. With the mixer on low speed, add the flour mixture and buttermilk alternately in two separate batches each. Beat on low speed for 2 minutes or until well combined. Fold in the walnuts.
4 Spoon 24 even tablespoonfuls of the mixture onto the baking sheets, leaving 2 inches between them to allow for spreading. Bake for 10–12 minutes, swapping the baking sheets around after 8 minutes, or until just firm to the touch. Allow to cool on baking sheets for 2 minutes then transfer to a cake rack to cool completely.
5 Use a ¾ inch star nozzle to pipe the cream cheese frosting onto the flat sides of half the whoopies. Place the extra chopped walnuts in a small bowl. Dip the frosted whoopies into the walnuts. Sandwich with the remaining whoopies. Pipe a small amount of the remaining frosting onto the top of each whoopie. Top with a walnut half.

Chocolate & walnut whoopies

Preparation time: 25 minutes
Cooking time: 11 minutes
Makes: 14

1 stick unsalted butter, just softened
⅓ cup (firmly packed) soft brown sugar
1 egg, at room temperature
1 teaspoon vanilla extract
1¼ cups all-purpose flour
1 tablespoon unsweetened cocoa powder
½ teaspoon baking powder
½ teaspoon baking soda
⅓ cup milk
½ cup chopped dark chocolate, melted, cooled
¾ quantity dark chocolate ganache (see page 122),
   well chilled
½ cup walnuts, toasted, finely chopped, to decorate

TIP: Keep filled whoopies in an airtight container in the fridge for up to 3 days. Serve at room temperature.

1 Preheat the oven to 350°F. Line three large baking sheets with baking paper.
2 Use an electric mixer to beat the butter and sugar in a medium bowl, scraping down the side as necessary, until pale and creamy. Add the egg and vanilla and beat well.
3 Sift the flour, cocoa, baking powder, and baking soda together. With the mixer on low speed, add the flour mixture and milk alternately in two separate batches each. Beat on low speed for 2 minutes or until well combined. Stir in the melted chocolate until just combined.

4 Spoon or pipe 28 x 1½ inch rounds of the mixture onto the baking sheets, leaving 2 inches between them. Bake for 11 minutes, swapping the baking sheets around after 8 minutes, or until just firm to the touch. Cool for 2 minutes on the baking sheets then transfer to a cake rack to cool completely.
5 Use an electric mixer to beat the chilled chocolate ganache in a small bowl for 1 minute or until slightly thickened and paler in color. Spread the ganache onto the flat sides of half the whoopies, spreading to the edges. Sandwich with the remaining whoopies. Roll the sides of the whoopies in the toasted walnuts to coat.

Vanilla & passion fruit whoopies

Preparation time: 25 minutes
Cooking time: 12 minutes
Makes: 8

1 stick unsalted butter, just softened
¾ cup superfine sugar
1 egg, at room temperature
1 teaspoon vanilla extract
2 cups all-purpose flour
1 teaspoon baking powder
½ teaspoon baking soda
⅔ cup milk
1 quantity vanilla buttercream (see page 118), made
    with 2 tablespoons fresh passion fruit pulp
confectioners' sugar, to dust

TIP: Keep filled whoopies in an airtight container in the fridge for up to 3 days. Serve at room temperature.

1 Preheat the oven to 350°F. Line three large baking sheets with baking paper.

2 Use an electric mixer to beat the butter and sugar in a medium bowl, scraping down the side as necessary, until pale and creamy. Add the egg and vanilla and beat well.

3 Sift the flour, baking powder, and baking soda together. With the mixer on low speed, add the flour mixture and milk alternately in two separate batches each. Beat on low speed for 2 minutes or until well combined.

4 Spoon 16 even, heaping tablespoonfuls of the mixture onto the baking sheets, leaving 2 inches between them to allow for spreading. Bake for 12 minutes, swapping the baking sheets around after 8 minutes, or until light golden and just firm to the touch. Cool for 2 minutes on the baking sheets then transfer to a cake rack to cool completely.

5 Spread or pipe the buttercream onto the flat sides of half the whoopies. Sandwich with the remaining whoopies. Dust with confectioners' sugar.

Lemon meringue whoopies

Preparation time: 30 minutes (+ cooling and chilling time)
Cooking time: 25 minutes
Makes: 18

1 stick unsalted butter, just softened
¾ cup superfine sugar
1 egg, at room temperature
1½ tablespoons finely grated lemon zest
1 teaspoon vanilla extract
2 cups all-purpose flour
1 teaspoon baking powder
½ teaspoon baking soda
⅔ cup buttermilk
⅔ quantity meringue frosting
   (see page 119)
confectioners' sugar, to dust

Lemon curd
2 tablespoons cornstarch, sifted
½ cup strained lemon juice
2 eggs, at room temperature,
   lightly beaten
¾ cup superfine sugar
1 stick unsalted butter, cubed

1 Preheat the oven to 350°F. Line three large baking sheets with baking paper.
2 Use an electric mixer to beat the butter and sugar in a medium bowl, scraping down the side as necessary, until pale and creamy. Add the egg, zest, and vanilla and beat well.
3 Sift the flour, baking powder, and baking soda together. With the mixer on low speed, add the flour mixture and buttermilk alternately in two separate batches each. Beat on low speed for 2 minutes or until well combined.
4 Spoon 36 even tablespoonfuls of mixture onto the baking sheets, leaving 2 inches between them. Bake for 10–12 minutes, swapping the sheets around after 8 minutes, or until light golden and just firm to the touch. Allow to cool for 2 minutes on the baking sheets then transfer to a cake rack to cool.
5 To make the lemon curd, mix the cornstarch with 2 tablespoons water in a small saucepan. Add the remaining ingredients and stir with a

whisk over low heat until the mixture thickens and just comes to a boil. Transfer to a heatproof bowl, cover the surface of the curd with plastic wrap, and cool to room temperature. Cover and refrigerate until well chilled.
6 Use a ¾ inch plain nozzle to pipe large dots of the meringue frosting onto the flat sides of half the whoopies. Use a ½ inch plain nozzle to pipe smaller amounts of the lemon curd between the frosting. Sandwich with the remaining whoopies. Dust with confectioners' sugar. Refrigerate, covered, for 30 minutes before serving.

TIP: Keep unfilled whoopies in an airtight container at room temperature for up to 3 days. They are best filled just before serving.

Honey whoopies

Preparation time: 20 minutes
Cooking time: 12 minutes
Makes: 14

1 stick unsalted butter, just softened
⅓ cup superfine sugar
2 tablespoons honey
1 egg, at room temperature
1 teaspoon vanilla extract
1½ cups all-purpose flour
½ teaspoon baking powder
1 teaspoon baking soda
½ cup buttermilk
⅓ cup flaked almonds

Honey buttercream
1½ sticks butter, just softened
1½ cups confectioners' sugar, sifted
2 tablespoons honey

> **TIP:** Keep filled whoopies in an airtight container in the fridge for up to 2 days. Serve at room temperature.

1 Preheat the oven to 350°F. Line three large baking sheets with baking paper.

2 Use an electric mixer to beat the butter, sugar, and honey in a medium bowl, scraping down the side as necessary, until pale and creamy. Add the egg and vanilla and beat well.

3 Sift the flour, baking powder, and baking soda together. With the mixer on low speed, add the flour mixture and buttermilk alternately in two separate batches each. Beat on low speed for 2 minutes or until well combined.

4 Use a ¾ inch plain nozzle to pipe 28 x 1¾ inch rounds of the mixture onto the baking sheets, leaving 2 inches between them to allow for spreading. Sprinkle half the rounds with the almonds. Bake for 12 minutes, swapping the baking sheets around after 8 minutes, or until light golden and just firm to the touch. Allow to cool for 2 minutes on the baking sheets then transfer to a cake rack to cool completely.

5 To make the honey buttercream, use an electric mixer to beat the butter until very smooth and pale. With the mixer on low speed, add the confectioners' sugar, ½ cup at a time, and beat well after each addition. When all the confectioners' sugar is incorporated, add the honey and beat on medium speed until well combined.

6 Use a ½ inch plain nozzle to pipe the honey buttercream onto the flat sides of the plain whoopies. Sandwich with the almond whoopies.

Playing
with flavors

Pistachio & rosewater whoopies

Preparation time: 35 minutes
Cooking time: 12 minutes
Makes: 18

1½ cups pistachio nuts
1 stick unsalted butter, just softened
¾ cup superfine sugar
1 egg, at room temperature
1 teaspoon vanilla extract
1¾ cups all-purpose flour
1 teaspoon baking powder
½ teaspoon baking soda
1 cup plus 1 tablespoon milk
1 tablespoon rosewater, or to taste
pink food coloring
1½ quantities vanilla buttercream (see page 118)
confectioners' sugar, to dust

TIP: Keep filled whoopies in an airtight container in the fridge for up to 3 days. Serve at room temperature.

1 Preheat the oven to 350°F. Line three large baking sheets with baking paper. Use a food processor to process the pistachios until very finely ground, then set aside.

2 Use an electric mixer to beat the butter and sugar in a medium bowl, scraping down the side as necessary, until pale and creamy. Add the egg and vanilla and beat well.

3 Sift the flour, baking powder, and baking soda together. With the mixer on low speed, add the flour mixture and milk alternately in two separate batches each. Add the pistachios then beat on low speed for 2 minutes or until well combined.

4 Use a ¾ inch plain nozzle to pipe 36 x 1¾ inch rounds of the mixture onto the baking sheets, leaving 2 inches between them to allow for spreading. Bake for 12 minutes, swapping the baking sheets around after 8 minutes, or until light golden and just firm to the touch. Allow to cool for 2 minutes on the baking sheets then transfer to a cake rack to cool completely.

5 Add the rosewater and a few drops of food coloring to the vanilla buttercream to tint it to the desired color and beat until combined. Use a ⅝ inch plain nozzle to pipe the buttercream onto the flat sides of half the whoopies. Sandwich with the remaining whoopies. Dust with confectioners' sugar.

Choc-mint whoopies

Preparation time: 30 minutes (+ 1 hour chilling time)
Cooking time: 10 minutes
Makes: 25

1 stick unsalted butter, just softened
¾ cup (lightly packed) soft brown sugar
1 egg, at room temperature
1 teaspoon vanilla extract
1½ cups all-purpose flour
⅔ cup unsweetened cocoa powder
1 teaspoon baking powder
½ teaspoon baking soda
⅔ cup milk
green food coloring
3 teaspoons peppermint extract, or to taste
⅔ quantity meringue frosting (see page 119)
3 x 1¼ ounce Peppermint Crisps (or similar mint
  chocolate confectionery), finely chopped

TIP: Keep unfilled whoopies in an airtight container at room temperature for up to 3 days. They are best filled just before serving.

1 Preheat the oven to 350°F. Line three large baking sheets with baking paper.
2 Use an electric mixer to beat the butter and sugar in a medium bowl, scraping down the side as necessary, until pale and creamy. Add the egg and vanilla and beat well.
3 Sift the flour, cocoa, baking powder, and baking soda together. With the mixer on low speed, add the flour mixture and milk alternately in two separate batches each. Beat on low speed until just combined. Cover and place in the fridge until firm.
4 Use damp hands to roll 50 even, heaping teaspoonfuls of the mixture into balls. Place the balls on the baking sheets, leaving 1¼ inches between them to allow for spreading. Bake for 8–10 minutes, swapping the baking sheets around after 6 minutes, or until just firm to the touch. (Do not overcook, or they will dry out.) Allow to cool for 2 minutes on the baking sheets then transfer to a cake rack to cool completely.
5 Stir a few drops of green food coloring through the meringue frosting to tint it to the desired color. Stir in the peppermint extract. Spread or use a ¾ inch plain nozzle to pipe the frosting onto the flat sides of half the whoopies, spreading to the edges. Sandwich with the remaining whoopies. Roll the sides of the whoopies in the chopped candy to coat.

White chocolate & raspberry whoopies

Preparation time: 35 minutes
Cooking time: 12 minutes
Makes: 30

1 stick unsalted butter, just softened
¾ cup superfine sugar
1 egg, at room temperature
1 teaspoon vanilla extract
2 cups all-purpose flour
1½ teaspoons baking powder
½ teaspoon baking soda
⅔ cup milk
heaping 1 cup chopped white chocolate
pink food coloring
1 quantity vanilla buttercream (see page 118)
2 cups raspberries
2 tablespoons sugar

TIP: Keep unfilled whoopies in an airtight container at room temperature for up to 3 days. They are best filled just before serving.

1 Preheat the oven to 350°F. Line three large baking sheets with baking paper.
2 Use an electric mixer to beat the butter and sugar in a medium bowl, scraping down the side as necessary, until pale and creamy. Add the egg and vanilla and beat well.
3 Sift the flour, baking powder, and baking soda together. With the mixer on low speed, add the flour mixture and milk alternately in two separate batches each. Beat on low speed until just combined. Fold in the white chocolate.
4 Spoon 60 heaping teaspoonfuls of the mixture onto the baking sheets, leaving 2 inches between them to allow for spreading. Bake for 10–12 minutes or until light golden

and just firm to the touch. (Do not open the oven door during cooking as this will affect the whoopies.) Allow to cool for 2 minutes on the baking sheets then transfer to a cake rack to cool completely.
5 Mix a few drops of the food coloring through the vanilla buttercream to tint it to the desired color. Spread or pipe the buttercream onto the flat sides of half the whoopies. Top each with four raspberries. Sandwich with the remaining whoopies, pressing lightly together.
6 Place the sugar and 1–2 drops of the pink food coloring in a jar or zip-lock bag and shake well until the sugar is evenly colored. Sprinkle the whoopies with the pink sugar.

Moist beet & chocolate whoopies

Preparation time: 35 minutes
Cooking time: 12 minutes
Makes: 22

1 stick unsalted butter, just softened
½ cup (firmly packed) soft brown sugar
1 egg, at room temperature
1 teaspoon vanilla extract
1 cup all-purpose flour
¼ cup unsweetened cocoa powder
1 teaspoon baking powder
½ teaspoon baking soda
⅓ cup milk
½ cup coarsely grated fresh beets
1 quantity chocolate buttercream (see page 118)

TIP: Keep filled whoopies in an airtight container in the fridge for up to 2 days. Serve at room temperature.

1 Preheat the oven to 350°F. Line three large baking sheets with baking paper.

2 Use an electric mixer to beat the butter and sugar in a medium bowl, scraping down the side as necessary, until pale and creamy. Add the egg and vanilla and beat well.

3 Sift the flour, cocoa, baking powder, and baking soda together. With the mixer on low speed, add the flour and milk alternately in two separate batches each. Beat on low speed for 2 minutes or until well combined. Fold through the beets.

4 Spoon 44 level tablespoonfuls of the mixture onto the baking sheets, leaving 2 inches between them to allow for spreading. Bake for 12 minutes, swapping the baking sheets around after 8 minutes, or until just firm to the touch. Allow to cool for 2 minutes on the baking sheets then transfer to a cake rack to cool completely.

5 Spread the flat sides of half the whoopies with the chocolate buttercream. Sandwich with the remaining whoopies.

Choc-top caramel whoopies

Preparation time: 30 minutes (+ setting time)
Cooking time: 12 minutes
Makes: 13

1 stick unsalted butter, just softened
¾ cup (lightly packed) dark brown sugar
1 egg, at room temperature
1 teaspoon vanilla extract
2 cups all-purpose flour
1 teaspoon baking powder
½ teaspoon baking soda
⅓ cup milk
12 ounces dark chocolate, melted
1 quantity chocolate buttercream (see page 118)

1 Preheat the oven to 350°F. Line three large baking sheets with baking paper.
2 Use an electric mixer to beat the butter and sugar in a medium bowl, scraping down the side as necessary, until pale and creamy. Add the egg and vanilla and beat well.
3 Sift the flour, baking powder, and baking soda together. With the mixer on low speed, add the flour mixture and milk alternately in two separate batches each. Beat on low speed for 2 minutes or until well combined.
4 Spoon 26 even tablespoonfuls of the mixture onto the baking sheets, leaving 2 inches between them to allow for spreading. Bake for 10–12 minutes, swapping the baking sheets around after 8 minutes, or until light golden and just firm to the touch. Allow to cool for 2 minutes on the baking sheets then transfer to a cake rack to cool completely.
5 Dip the tops of half the whoopies into the melted chocolate to coat and set aside to set. Once set, spread or pipe the chocolate buttercream onto the flat sides of the remaining whoopies and sandwich with the chocolate-coated whoopies.

TIP: Keep filled whoopies in an airtight container in the fridge for up to 3 days. Serve at room temperature.

Tiramisu whoopies

Preparation time: 25 minutes
Cooking time: 12 minutes
Makes: 22

1½ tablespoons instant coffee granules
¼ cup Marsala
1 stick unsalted butter, just softened
¾ cup superfine sugar
1 egg, at room temperature
2 cups all-purpose flour
1 teaspoon baking powder
½ teaspoon baking soda
¼ cup milk
1 tablespoon unsweetened cocoa powder, sifted
1 quantity cream cheese frosting (see page 121)
⅔ cup chopped dark chocolate, melted, cooled

> **TIP:** The cocoa powder can be dusted on after sandwiching the whoopies, for a different look.
>
> Keep filled whoopies in an airtight container in the fridge for up to 3 days. Stand at room temperature for 15 minutes before serving.

1 Preheat the oven to 350°F. Line three large baking sheets with baking paper.

2 Place the coffee granules in a small bowl and mix with 1½ tablespoons of boiling water to dissolve. Stir in the Marsala. Set aside to cool.

3 Use an electric mixer to beat the butter and sugar in a medium bowl, scraping down the side as necessary, until pale and creamy. Add the egg and beat well.

4 Sift the flour, baking powder, and baking soda together. With the mixer on low speed, add the flour mixture and milk alternately in two separate batches each, followed by the cooled coffee mixture. Beat on low speed for 2 minutes or until well combined.

5 Spoon 44 even tablespoonfuls of the mixture onto the baking sheets, leaving 2 inches between them to allow for spreading. Lightly dust the whoopies with the cocoa. Bake for 10–12 minutes, swapping the baking sheets around after 8 minutes, or until light golden and just firm to the touch. Allow to cool for 2 minutes on the baking sheets then transfer to a cake rack to cool completely.

6 Spread or pipe the cream cheese frosting onto the flat sides of half the whoopies. Spread the flat sides of the remaining whoopies with the melted chocolate and sandwich with the frosted whoopies.

Green tea & cherry whoopies

Preparation time: 35 minutes (+ 1 hour standing time)
Cooking time: 11 minutes
Makes: 16

3 green-tea bags
1 stick unsalted butter, just softened
¾ cup superfine sugar
1 egg, at room temperature
1 teaspoon vanilla extract
2 cups all-purpose flour
1 teaspoon baking powder
½ teaspoon baking soda
green food coloring
½ x 14 ounce can or jar pitted cherries in syrup,
  drained, syrup reserved
½ quantity vanilla buttercream (see page 118)
16 cherries, with stalks on (optional), to decorate

TIP: Keep filled whoopies in an airtight container in the fridge for up to 3 days. Decorate with the fresh cherries and serve at room temperature.

1 Combine the tea bags and ½ cup boiling water in a small bowl, cover, and stand for 1 hour to steep. Remove the tea bags, squeezing out as much liquid as possible, then discard the bags.

2 Preheat the oven to 350°F. Line three large baking sheets with baking paper.

3 Use an electric mixer to beat the butter and sugar in a medium bowl, scraping down the side as necessary, until pale and creamy. Add the egg and vanilla and beat well.

4 Sift the flour, baking powder, and baking soda together. With the mixer on low speed, add the flour mixture and cooled tea alternately in two separate batches each. Beat on low speed for 2 minutes or until well combined. Stir in a few drops of food coloring to tint the mixture pale green.

5 Use a ¾ inch plain nozzle to pipe 32 x 1½ inch rounds of the mixture onto the baking sheets, leaving 2 inches between them to allow for spreading. Bake for 11 minutes, swapping the baking sheets around after 8 minutes, or until light golden and firm to the touch. Allow to cool for 2 minutes on the baking sheets then transfer to a cake rack to cool completely.

6 Coarsely chop the tinned cherries. Beat the vanilla buttercream and 1 tablespoon of cherry syrup until combined. Use a ¾ inch plain nozzle to pipe the buttercream onto the flat side of half the whoopies. Top with the chopped cherries then sandwich with the remaining whoopies. Pipe a small round of the remaining buttercream on top of each whoopie then decorate with a whole cherry, if using.

Salted caramel & peanut whoopies

Preparation time: 35 minutes (+ cooling and 30 minutes chilling time)
Cooking time: 22 minutes
Makes: 16

⅓ cup unsalted butter, just softened
⅓ cup (firmly packed) soft brown sugar
1 egg, at room temperature
1 teaspoon vanilla extract
1⅓ cups all-purpose flour
½ teaspoon baking powder
1 teaspoon baking soda
⅓ cup milk
½ cup salted toasted peanuts, coarsely chopped

Salted caramel filling
14 ounce can sweetened condensed milk
½ cup (firmly packed) soft brown sugar
scant ⅓ cup butter, cubed
2 tablespoons light treacle or maple syrup
½–1 teaspoon salt, or to taste
2½ tablespoons whipping cream

TIP: Keep filled whoopies in an airtight container in the fridge for up to 3 days. Serve at room temperature.

1 Preheat the oven to 350°F. Line three large baking sheets with baking paper.

2 Use an electric mixer to beat the butter and sugar in a medium bowl, scraping down the side as necessary, until pale and creamy. Add the egg and vanilla and beat well.

3 Sift the flour, baking powder, and baking soda together. With the mixer on low speed, add the flour and milk alternately in two separate batches each. Beat on low speed for 2 minutes or until well combined.

4 Use a ¾ inch plain nozzle to pipe 32 x 1½ inch rounds of the mixture onto the baking sheets, leaving 2 inches between them. Bake for 10–12 minutes, swapping the baking sheets around after 8 minutes, or until light golden

and just firm to the touch. Cool for 2 minutes on the baking sheets then transfer to a cake rack to cool completely.

5 To make the filling, stir the condensed milk, sugar, butter, and treacle or syrup in a heavy-based saucepan over low heat until the sugar dissolves. Bring to a simmer, stirring constantly, for 8–10 minutes or until the mixture thickens and darkens. Stir in the salt and cream. Set aside until lukewarm.

6 Spread the filling onto the flat sides of half the whoopies, spreading to the edges. Sandwich with the remaining whoopies. Roll the sides of the whoopies in the chopped peanuts to coat. Refrigerate for 30 minutes before serving.

Caramel walnut whoopies

Preparation time: 40 minutes
Cooking time: 12 minutes
Makes: 7

1½ cups walnut pieces
1 stick unsalted butter, just softened
¾ cup (firmly packed) soft brown sugar
1 egg, at room temperature
1 teaspoon vanilla extract
2 cups all-purpose flour
1 teaspoon baking powder
½ teaspoon baking soda
½ cup milk
1 quantity vanilla buttercream (see page 118), made
    with 1 cup (lightly packed) soft brown sugar instead
    of 1 cup of the confectioners' sugar
⅔ cup chopped dark chocolate, melted

TIP: Keep filled whoopies in an airtight container in the fridge for up to 3 days. Serve at room temperature.

1 Preheat the oven to 350°F. Line three large baking sheets with baking paper.

2 Process the walnuts in a food processor using a pulse action until very finely ground. Set aside.

3 Use an electric mixer to beat the butter and sugar in a medium bowl, scraping down the side as necessary, until pale and creamy. Add the egg and vanilla and beat well.

4 Sift the flour, baking powder, and baking soda together. Stir in the walnuts. With the mixer on low speed, add the flour mixture and milk alternately in two separate batches each. Beat on low speed for about 2 minutes or until well combined.

5 Use a ¾ inch plain nozzle to pipe 14 x 2¾ inch rounds of the mixture onto the baking sheets, leaving 2 inches between them to allow for spreading. Bake for 10–12 minutes, swapping the baking sheets around halfway through cooking, or until light golden and just firm to the touch. Allow to cool for 2 minutes on the baking sheets then transfer to a cake rack to cool completely.

6 Use a ½ inch star nozzle to pipe the vanilla buttercream onto the flat sides of half the whoopies. Sandwich with the remaining whoopies. Use a knife or fork to drizzle melted chocolate over the tops of the whoopies.

Sweet polenta whoopies with honey & rosemary buttercream

Preparation time: 35 minutes
Cooking time: 12 minutes
Makes: 12

1 stick unsalted butter, just softened
¾ cup superfine sugar
1 egg, at room temperature
1 teaspoon vanilla extract
1¾ cups all-purpose flour
1 teaspoon baking powder
½ teaspoon baking soda
1 cup polenta
½ cup plus 1 tablespoon milk
1 cup flaked almonds, toasted, lightly crushed
confectioners' sugar and rosemary leaves, to decorate

Honey & rosemary buttercream
½ stick butter, just softened
⅓ cup honey
1⅔ cups firm, fresh ricotta cheese
1 tablespoon finely chopped rosemary leaves

TIP: Keep filled whoopies in an airtight container in the fridge for up to 1 day. Stand at room temperature for 15 minutes before serving.

1 Preheat the oven to 350°F. Line three large baking sheets with baking paper.

2 Use an electric mixer to beat the butter and sugar in a medium bowl, scraping down the side as necessary, until pale and creamy. Add the egg and vanilla and beat well.

3 Sift the flour, baking powder, and baking soda together. Stir in the polenta. With the mixer on low speed, add the flour mixture and milk alternately in two separate batches each. Beat on low speed for 2 minutes or until well combined.

4 Use a ¾ inch plain nozzle to pipe 24 x 2½ inch rounds of the mixture onto the baking sheets, leaving 2 inches between them to allow for spreading. Bake for 10–12 minutes, swapping the baking sheets around after 6 minutes, or until light golden and just firm to the touch. Allow to cool for 2 minutes on the baking sheets then transfer to a cake rack to cool completely.

5 To make the honey and rosemary buttercream, process all the ingredients in a food processor until smooth. Spread the buttercream on the flat sides of half the whoopies, spreading to the edges. Sandwich with the remaining whoopies. Roll the sides of the whoopies in the almonds to coat. Dust with confectioners' sugar and decorate with a few rosemary leaves.

Whoopies
for kids

Rainbow whoopies

Preparation time: 35 minutes
Cooking time: 8 minutes
Makes: 13

⅓ cup unsalted butter, just softened
⅓ cup superfine sugar
1 egg, at room temperature
1 teaspoon vanilla extract
1 cup all-purpose flour
½ teaspoon baking powder
¼ teaspoon baking soda
¼ cup milk
¼ quantity vanilla buttercream (see page 118)
½ quantity vanilla glaze (see page 120)
3 or 4 food colorings of your choice
decorations of your choice (see tip)

TIP: Sprinkles, heart sugar sprinkles, regular or mini M&Ms, and colored sugar all work well as decorations.

Keep filled (but undecorated) whoopies in an airtight container in the fridge for up to 3 days. They are best decorated on the day of serving. Serve at room temperature.

1 Preheat the oven to 350°F. Line three large baking sheets with baking paper.

2 Use an electric mixer to beat the butter and sugar in a medium bowl, scraping down the side as necessary, until pale and creamy. Add the egg and vanilla and beat well.

3 Sift the flour, baking powder, and baking soda together. With the mixer on low speed, add the flour mixture and milk alternately in two separate batches each. Beat on low speed for 2 minutes or until well combined.

4 Use a ¾ inch plain nozzle to pipe 26 x 1½ inch rounds of the mixture onto the baking sheets, leaving 2 inches between them. Bake for 8 minutes, swapping the baking sheets around after 6 minutes, or until light golden and just firm to the touch. Cool for 2 minutes on the baking sheets then transfer to a cake rack to cool completely.

5 Spread or pipe the vanilla buttercream over the flat sides of half the whoopies. Sandwich with the remaining whoopies.

6 Divide the vanilla glaze among three or four small bowls. Tint each one a different color with the food coloring. Spoon the glaze over the whoopie tops so that it drizzles down the sides a little. Sprinkle with decorations. Set aside until the glaze sets.

Rocky road whoopies

Preparation time: 25 minutes
Cooking time: 12 minutes
Makes: 14

1 stick unsalted butter, just softened
½ cup (firmly packed) soft brown sugar
1 egg, at room temperature
1 teaspoon vanilla extract
1 cup all-purpose flour
¼ cup unsweetened cocoa powder
½ teaspoon baking powder
½ teaspoon baking soda
½ cup milk
1 quantity milk chocolate ganache (see page 122),
   well chilled
⅔ cup grated dried coconut
⅔ cup mini marshmallows, halved
½ cup candied cherries, finely chopped

TIP: Keep unfilled whoopies in an airtight container at room temperature for up to 3 days. They are best filled and decorated on the day of serving.

1 Preheat the oven to 350°F. Line three large baking sheets with baking paper.
2 Use an electric mixer to beat the butter and sugar in a medium bowl, scraping down the side as necessary, until pale and creamy. Add the egg and vanilla and beat well.
3 Sift the flour, cocoa, baking powder, and baking soda together. With the mixer on low speed, add the flour mixture and milk alternately in two separate batches each. Beat on low speed for 2 minutes or until well combined.
4 Use a ⅝ inch plain nozzle to pipe 28 x 1¾ inch rounds of the mixture onto the baking sheets, leaving 2 inches between them to allow for spreading. Bake for 12 minutes, swapping the baking sheets around after 8 minutes, or until just firm to the touch. Allow to cool for 2 minutes on the baking sheets then transfer to a cake rack to cool completely.
5 Use an electric mixer to beat the ganache in a small bowl until pale and fluffy. Spread the ganache onto the flat sides of half the whoopies, spreading to the edges. Sandwich with the remaining whoopies. Combine the coconut, marshmallows, and cherries. Roll the sides of the whoopies in the coconut mixture to coat.

Doughnut whoopies

Preparation time: 30 minutes
Cooking time: 8 minutes
Makes: 15

½ cup vegetable oil
1 cup superfine sugar
1 egg, at room temperature
2 teaspoons vanilla extract
2 cups all-purpose flour
1 teaspoon baking powder
½ teaspoon baking soda
1½ teaspoons ground cinnamon
1 pinch salt
¼ cup milk
½ stick unsalted butter, melted
2 cups heavy cream
⅓ cup confectioners' sugar
½ cup strawberry jam

TIP: Keep unfilled whoopies in an airtight container at room temperature for up to 2 days. They are best filled just before serving. These whoopies are unsuitable to freeze.

1 Preheat the oven to 350°F. Line three large baking sheets with baking paper. Use a 1 inch round cutter to trace 30 circles, 2 inches apart, on the baking paper then turn the paper over.
2 Use an electric mixer to beat the oil, ⅔ cup of the superfine sugar, the egg, and 1 teaspoon of the vanilla in a medium bowl until combined. Sift the flour, baking powder, baking soda, 1 teaspoon of the cinnamon, and salt together. With the mixer on low speed, add the flour mixture and milk alternately in two separate batches each and beat until just combined.
3 Use a ½ inch plain nozzle to pipe the mixture into doughnut shapes outside the marked circles (they will spread as they cook) on the baking sheets. Bake for 8 minutes, swapping the baking sheets around after 6 minutes, or until light golden and just firm to the touch. (Do not overcook, or they will become dry.) Allow to cool for 2 minutes on the baking sheets then transfer to a cake rack to cool completely.
4 In a small bowl, combine the remaining cinnamon and sugar. Brush the tops of the warm whoopies liberally with the melted butter and dip into the sugar mixture to coat.
5 Use an electric mixer to whisk the cream, confectioners' sugar, and remaining vanilla in a medium bowl until firm peaks form. Spread a little less than 1 tablespoon of the jam onto the flat sides of half the whoopies. Use a ⅝ inch plain nozzle to pipe the whipped cream over the jam. Sandwich with the remaining whoopies.

Choc-malt & oat whoopies

Preparation time: 35 minutes
Cooking time: 12 minutes
Makes: 16

1 stick unsalted butter, just softened
⅔ cup (lightly packed) soft brown sugar
2½ tablespoons malt extract
1 egg, at room temperature
1 teaspoon vanilla extract
2 cups all-purpose flour
1 teaspoon baking powder
½ teaspoon baking soda
1 cup quick-cooking oats, plus extra,
　for sprinkling
½ cup milk
½ cup sour cream
1 quantity milk chocolate ganache (see page 122),
　made with 1 cup whipping cream and 2 tablespoons
　malt extract

TIP: Keep filled whoopies in an airtight container in the fridge for up to 3 days. Serve at room temperature.

1 Preheat the oven to 350°F. Line three large baking sheets with baking paper.
2 Use an electric mixer to beat the butter, sugar, and malt extract in a medium bowl, scraping down the side as necessary, until pale and creamy. Add the egg and vanilla and beat until well combined.
3 Sift the flour, baking powder, and baking soda together. Stir in the oats. With the mixer on low speed, add the flour mixture, milk, and sour cream alternately in two separate batches each. Beat on low speed for 2 minutes or until well combined.

4 Spoon 32 even, heaping tablespoonfuls of the mixture onto the baking sheets, leaving 2 inches between them to allow for spreading. Sprinkle half the whoopies with the extra oats. Bake for 12 minutes, swapping the baking sheets around after 8 minutes, or until light golden and just firm to the touch. Allow to cool for 2 minutes on the baking sheets then transfer to a cake rack to cool completely.
5 Use a palette knife to spread the flat sides of the plain whoopies with the ganache. Sandwich with the remaining whoopies.

Cinnamon party whoopies

Preparation time: 35 minutes (+ setting time)
Cooking time: 15 minutes
Makes: 12

1 stick unsalted butter, just softened
½ cup (firmly packed) soft brown sugar
1 egg, at room temperature
1 teaspoon vanilla extract
1½ cups all-purpose flour
2 teaspoons ground cinnamon
½ teaspoon baking powder
1 teaspoon baking soda
⅔ cup buttermilk
½ quantity vanilla buttercream (see page 118)
1 quantity royal icing (see page 121)
4 food colorings of your choice

TIP: Keep filled (but undecorated) whoopies in an airtight container in the fridge for up to 3 days. They are best decorated on the day of serving. Serve at room temperature.

1 Preheat the oven to 350°F. Line three large baking sheets with baking paper.

2 Use an electric mixer to beat the butter and sugar in a medium bowl, scraping down the side as necessary, until pale and creamy. Add the egg and vanilla and beat well.

3 Sift the flour, cinnamon, baking powder, and baking soda together. With the mixer on low speed, add the flour mixture and buttermilk alternately in two separate batches each. Beat on low speed for 2 minutes or until well combined.

4 Use a ¾ inch plain nozzle to pipe 24 x 2½ inch rounds of the mixture onto the baking sheets, leaving 2 inches between them to

allow for spreading. Bake for 10–15 minutes, swapping the baking sheets around halfway through cooking, or until light golden and just firm to the touch. Allow to cool for 2 minutes on the baking sheets then transfer to a cake rack to cool completely.

5 Pipe or spread the vanilla buttercream onto the flat sides of half the whoopies. Sandwich with the remaining whoopies.

6 Divide the royal icing among four bowls and tint each one a desired color. Spoon each color into a separate zip-lock bag. Snip off a corner from each bag to make a small hole and pipe designs over the whoopie tops as desired. Set aside until the icing sets.

Ice cream whoopies

Preparation time: 35 minutes (+ 2 hours freezing time)
Cooking time: 8 minutes
Makes: 20

8 cups vanilla ice cream
1 stick unsalted butter, just softened
¾ cup (lightly packed) soft brown sugar
1 egg, at room temperature
1 teaspoon vanilla extract
1½ cups all-purpose flour
⅔ cup unsweetened cocoa powder
1 teaspoon baking powder
½ teaspoon baking soda
⅔ cup milk
various sugar sprinkles of your choice, to decorate

TIP: Keep unfilled whoopies in an airtight container in the fridge for up to 3 days. They are best filled just before serving. Serve at room temperature.

1 Preheat the oven to 350°F. Line three large baking sheets with baking paper. Spray a 12 x 7 inch baking pan with oil spray and line with plastic wrap, allowing it to overhang the sides.
2 Scoop the ice cream into a bowl and let it stand at room temperature for 10 minutes, or until softened slightly. Spoon into the lined baking pan. Cover with a piece of baking paper and press down firmly to flatten evenly. Place in the freezer for 2 hours or until frozen.
3 Use an electric mixer to beat the butter and sugar in a medium bowl, scraping down the side as necessary, until pale and creamy. Add the egg and vanilla and beat well.
4 Sift the flour, cocoa, baking powder, and baking soda together. With the mixer on low speed, add the flour mixture and milk alternately in two separate batches each. Beat on low speed until well combined.

5 Use a ¾ inch plain nozzle to pipe 40 x 1½ inch rounds of the mixture onto the baking sheets, leaving 1¼ inches between them to allow for spreading. Bake for 8 minutes, swapping the sheets around after 6 minutes, or until just firm to the touch. (Do not overcook, or they will dry out.) Allow to cool for 2 minutes on the baking sheets then transfer to a cake rack to cool completely.
6 Place the sugar sprinkles in separate bowls. Use a 1¾ inch round cutter to cut out 1 round of ice cream. Roll the sides in the sugar sprinkles. Place on a baking sheet lined with baking paper and transfer to the freezer. Repeat with the remaining ice cream and sprinkles until you have 20 in total.
7 To serve, sandwich each ice cream round between the flat sides of two whoopies. Serve immediately.

Choc-honeycomb whoopies

Preparation time: 20 minutes
Cooking time: 12 minutes
Makes: 13

1 stick unsalted butter, just softened
½ cup (firmly packed) soft brown sugar
1 egg, at room temperature
1 teaspoon vanilla extract
1 cup all-purpose flour
⅓ cup unsweetened cocoa powder
1 teaspoon baking powder
½ teaspoon baking soda
½ cup milk
1¼ cups whipping cream
2 x 1¾ ounce chocolate-coated honeycomb
  bars, finely chopped

TIP: Keep unfilled whoopies in an airtight container in the fridge for up to 3 days. They are best filled just before serving. Serve at room temperature.

1 Preheat the oven to 350°F. Line three large baking sheets with baking paper.
2 Use an electric mixer to beat the butter and sugar in a medium bowl, scraping down the side as necessary, until pale and creamy. Add the egg and vanilla and beat well.
3 Sift the flour, cocoa, baking powder, and baking soda together. With the mixer on low speed, add the flour mixture and milk alternately in two separate batches each. Beat on low speed for 2 minutes or until well combined.
4 Use a ¾ inch plain nozzle to pipe 26 x 1½ inch rounds of the mixture onto the baking sheets, leaving 2 inches between them to allow for spreading. Bake for 12 minutes, swapping the sheets around after 8 minutes, or until light golden and just firm to the touch. Allow to cool for 2 minutes on the baking sheets then transfer to a cake rack to cool completely.
5 Use an electric mixer to whisk the cream until firm peaks form. Fold half the chocolate-coated honeycomb through the whipped cream. Spread the cream mixture onto the flat sides of half the whoopies, spreading to the edges. Sandwich with the remaining whoopies. Roll the sides of the whoopies in the remaining chocolate-coated honeycomb to coat.

Christening whoopies

Preparation time: 1 hour 20 minutes (+ 3 hours standing time)
Cooking time: 12 minutes
Makes: 15

1 stick unsalted butter, just softened
¾ cup superfine sugar
1 egg, at room temperature
1 teaspoon vanilla extract
½ teaspoon almond extract
1¾ cups all-purpose flour
1 teaspoon baking powder
½ teaspoon baking soda
1 cup ground almonds
½ cup milk
1 quantity vanilla glaze (see page 120)
pink and/or blue food coloring
½ quantity royal icing (see page 121)
cachous, to decorate
1 quantity white chocolate ganache
(see page 122), well chilled

TIP: Keep unfilled and undecorated whoopies in an airtight container at room temperature for up to 2 days. They are best filled and decorated on the day of serving.

1 Preheat the oven to 350°F. Line three large baking sheets with baking paper.
2 Use an electric mixer to beat the butter and sugar in a medium bowl, scraping down the sides, until pale and creamy. Add the egg, vanilla, and almond extract and beat well.
3 Sift the flour, baking powder, and baking soda together. Stir in the ground almonds. With the mixer on low speed, add the flour mixture and milk alternately in two separate batches each. Beat on low speed for 2 minutes or until well combined.
4 Spoon 30 slightly heaping tablespoonfuls of mixture onto the baking sheets, leaving 2 inches between them. Bake for 10–12 minutes, swapping sheets around halfway through cooking, or until light golden and just firm to the

touch. Cool for 2 minutes on the baking sheets then transfer to a cake rack to cool completely.
5 Divide the glaze between two bowls and add enough food coloring to tint to the desired color. Use a flat-bladed knife to ice the tops of half the whoopies then set aside on a cake rack for 2 hours or until the glaze is completely set.
6 Spoon the royal icing into a zip-lock bag and cut a small hole in one of the corners. Pipe a wiggly pattern over the top of the iced whoopies. Decorate with the cachous. Set the whoopies aside for 1 hour or until glaze is set.
7 Use electric beaters to beat the ganache for 2–3 minutes until thick. Use a ¾ inch plain nozzle to pipe the ganache onto the flat sides of the un-iced whoopies. Sandwich with the iced whoopies (take care to not damage decorations).

Banana split whoopies

Preparation time: 25 minutes
Cooking time: 12 minutes
Makes: 12

1 stick unsalted butter, just softened
1 cup (firmly packed) soft brown sugar
1 egg, at room temperature
1 teaspoon vanilla extract
2 cups all-purpose flour
1½ teaspoons baking powder
½ teaspoon baking soda
½ cup mashed ripe banana (see tip)
⅓ cup buttermilk
½ quantity marshmallow frosting (see page 123)
⅔ cup chopped dark chocolate, melted
1¼ cup crushed nuts (optional)

TIP: You will need 1 large ripe banana for this recipe.

Keep unfilled and undecorated whoopies in an airtight container at room temperature for up to 2 days. They are best filled and decorated just before serving.

1 Preheat the oven to 350°F. Line three large baking sheets with baking paper.
2 Use an electric mixer to beat the butter and sugar in a medium bowl, scraping down the side as necessary, until pale and creamy. Add the egg and vanilla and beat well.
3 Sift the flour, baking powder, and baking soda together. With the mixer on low speed, add the flour mixture, mashed banana, and buttermilk alternately in two separate batches each. Beat on low speed until just combined.
4 Use a ¾ inch plain nozzle to pipe 24 banana shapes (about 3½ inches long and ¾ inch wide) of the mixture onto the baking sheets, leaving 2 inches between them to allow for spreading. Bake for 12 minutes, swapping the baking sheets around after 8 minutes, until light golden and just firm to the touch. Allow to cool for 2 minutes on the baking sheets then transfer to a cake rack to cool completely.
5 Spread or pipe the warm marshmallow frosting onto the flat sides of half the whoopies. Sandwich with the remaining whoopies. Spoon the melted chocolate over the top of the whoopies to decorate and sprinkle with the nuts, if using.

Alphabet whoopies

Preparation time: 1 hour 20 minutes (+ 3 hours standing time)
Cooking time: 12 minutes
Makes: 12

1 stick unsalted butter, just softened
¾ cup superfine sugar
1 tablespoon finely grated orange zest
1 egg, at room temperature
1 teaspoon vanilla extract
½ teaspoon almond extract
1¾ cups all-purpose flour
1 teaspoon baking powder
½ teaspoon baking soda
1 cup ground almonds
⅓ cup milk
1 quantity vanilla glaze (see page 120),
   tinted to desired color
½ quantity royal icing (see page 121),
   tinted to desired color
1 quantity vanilla buttercream (see page 118)

> **TIP:** Keep unfilled and undecorated whoopies in an airtight container at room temperature for up to 2 days. They are best filled and decorated on the day of serving.

1 Preheat the oven to 350°F. Line three large baking sheets with baking paper.
2 Use an electric mixer to beat the butter, sugar, and orange zest in a medium bowl, scraping down the side as necessary, until pale and creamy. Add the egg, vanilla, and almond extract and beat well.
3 Sift the flour, baking powder, and baking soda together. Stir in the ground almonds. With the mixer on low speed, add the flour mixture and milk alternately in two separate batches each. Beat on low speed for 2 minutes or until well combined.
4 Spoon 24 even, slightly heaping table-spoonfuls of the mixture onto the baking sheets, leaving 2 inches between them. Bake for 10–12 minutes, swapping the baking sheets

around after 8 minutes, or until light golden and just firm to the touch. Allow to cool for 2 minutes on the baking sheets then transfer to a cake rack to cool completely.
5 Use a flat-bladed knife to spread the glaze over the tops of half the whoopies. Set aside on a cake rack for 2 hours or until set.
6 Spoon the royal icing into a zip-lock bag and cut a small hole in one of the corners. Pipe letters (or names or numbers) on the tops of the iced whoopies. Set aside on a cake rack for 1 hour or until the glaze is set.
7 Use a ¾ inch plain nozzle to pipe the buttercream onto the flat sides of the un-iced whoopies. Sandwich with the iced whoopies (take care to not damage the decorations).

Chocolate caramel whoopies

Preparation time: 35 minutes
Cooking time: 12 minutes
Makes: 15

⅓ cup unsalted butter, just softened
2 tablespoons soft brown sugar
2 tablespoons light treacle or maple syrup
1 egg, at room temperature
1 teaspoon vanilla extract
1 cup all-purpose flour
½ teaspoon baking powder
½ teaspoon baking soda
⅓ cup milk
1⅓ cups dark chocolate melts, melted
1 quantity chocolate buttercream (see page 118)

TIP: Keep unfilled and undecorated whoopies in an airtight container at room temperature for up to 2 days. They are best filled and decorated on the day of serving.

1 Preheat the oven to 350°F. Line three large baking sheets with baking paper.
2 Use an electric mixer to beat the butter, sugar, and treacle or syrup in a medium bowl, scraping down the side as necessary, until pale and creamy. Add the egg and vanilla extract and beat well.
3 Sift the flour, baking powder, and baking soda together. With the mixer on low speed, add the flour mixture and milk alternately in two separate batches each. Beat on low speed for 2 minutes or until well combined.
4 Spoon 30 even, level tablespoonfuls of the mixture onto the baking sheets, leaving 2 inches between them to allow for spreading.

Bake for 10–12 minutes, swapping the baking sheets around halfway through cooking, or until light golden and just firm to the touch. Allow to cool for 2 minutes on the baking sheets then transfer to a cake rack to cool completely.
5 Dip half of each whoopie into the melted chocolate. Place on a baking paper-lined baking sheet until set.
6 Use a ⅝ inch star nozzle to pipe the buttercream onto the flat sides of half the whoopies. Sandwich with the remaining whoopies with the chocolate-coated sides facing the same way.

Whoopies for grownups

Espresso chocolate whoopies

Preparation time: 50 minutes
Cooking time: 10 minutes
Makes: 22

1 stick unsalted butter, just softened
¾ cup (firmly packed) soft brown sugar
1 egg, at room temperature
1½ teaspoons vanilla extract
2 cups all-purpose flour
1 teaspoon baking powder
½ teaspoon baking soda
¼ cup very finely ground coffee beans
½ cup milk
1 quantity dark chocolate ganache (see page 122)
22 coffee beans (optional), to decorate

TIP: Keep filled and decorated whoopies in an airtight container in the fridge for up to 3 days. Stand at room temperature for 30 minutes before serving.

1 Preheat the oven to 350°F. Line three large baking sheets with baking paper.
2 Use an electric mixer to beat the butter and sugar in a medium bowl, scraping down the side as necessary, until pale and creamy. Add the egg and vanilla and beat well.
3 Sift the flour, baking powder, baking soda, and coffee together. With the mixer on low speed, add the flour mixture and milk alternately in two separate batches each. Beat on low speed for 2 minutes or until well combined.
4 Use a ⅝ inch plain nozzle to pipe 44 x 1½ inch rounds of the mixture onto the baking sheets, leaving 1¼ inches between them to allow for spreading. Bake for 10 minutes, swapping the baking sheets around halfway through cooking, or until just firm to the touch. Allow to cool for 2 minutes on the baking sheets then transfer to a cake rack to cool completely.
5 Use a ½ inch star nozzle to pipe the chocolate ganache onto the flat sides of half the whoopies. Sandwich with the remaining whoopies. Pipe a rosette, using the remaining ganache, on top of each whoopie then decorate each with a coffee bean, if using.

Frangelico & lime whoopies

Preparation time: 25 minutes
Cooking time: 15 minutes
Makes: 14

1 stick unsalted butter, just softened
¾ cup superfine sugar
1 egg, at room temperature
1½ cups all-purpose flour
1 teaspoon baking powder
½ teaspoon baking soda
heaping ½ cup ground hazelnuts
¼ cup Frangelico liqueur
1 quantity vanilla buttercream (see page 118),
   made with 2 tablespoons finely grated lime zest
confectioners' sugar, to dust

1 Preheat the oven to 350°F. Line three large baking sheets with baking paper.
2 Use an electric mixer to beat the butter and sugar in a medium bowl, scraping down the side as necessary, until pale and creamy. Add the egg and beat well.
3 Sift the flour, baking powder, and baking soda together. With the mixer on low speed, add the flour, ground hazelnuts, and Frangelico alternately in two separate batches. Beat on low speed until just combined.
4 Spoon 28 even tablespoonfuls of the mixture onto the baking sheets, leaving 2 inches between them to allow for spreading. Bake for 12–15 minutes or until light golden and just firm to the touch. Allow to cool for 2 minutes on the baking sheets then transfer to a cake rack to cool completely.
5 Spread or pipe the buttercream onto the flat sides of half the whoopies. Sandwich with the remaining whoopies. Dust with confectioners' sugar.

TIP: Keep filled whoopies in an airtight container in the fridge for up to 3 days. Stand at room temperature for 30 minutes before serving.

Raspberry & white chocolate cheesecake whoopie hearts

Preparation time: 30 minutes
Cooking time: 12 minutes
Makes: 9

1 stick unsalted butter, just softened,
 plus extra, melted, for greasing
¾ cup superfine sugar
3 teaspoons finely grated lemon zest
1 teaspoon vanilla extract
1 egg, at room temperature
2 cups all-purpose flour
1 teaspoon baking powder
½ teaspoon baking soda
⅔ cup milk
⅔ cup chopped white chocolate, melted, cooled
½ quantity cream cheese frosting (see page 121)
⅔ cup raspberries
confectioners' sugar, to dust

> **TIP:** Keep filled whoopies in an airtight container in the fridge for up to 2 days. Stand at room temperature for 30 minutes before serving. Dust with confectioners' sugar just before serving.

1 Preheat the oven to 190°C (375°F/Gas 5). Lightly brush three six-hole 3½ inch x 3¼ inch heart pans with butter to grease.

2 Use an electric mixer to beat the butter, sugar, lemon zest, and vanilla in a medium bowl, scraping down the side as necessary, until pale and creamy. Add the egg and beat well.

3 Sift the flour, baking powder, and baking soda together. With the mixer on low speed, add the flour mixture and milk alternately in two separate batches each. Beat on medium speed for 2 minutes or until well combined.

4 Divide the mixture evenly among the pans and use the back of a teaspoon to smooth the surfaces. Bake for 10–12 minutes, swapping the tins around after 8 minutes, or until light golden and just firm to the touch. Allow to cool for 2 minutes in the tins then turn onto a cake rack to cool completely.

5 Meanwhile, use an electric mixer to beat the cooled white chocolate through the cream cheese frosting. Stir through the raspberries, crushing them lightly. Cover and refrigerate until firm.

6 Spread the chilled raspberry filling onto the flat sides of half the whoopies. Sandwich with the remaining whoopies. Dust with confectioners' sugar.

Black forest whoopies

Preparation time: 30 minutes
Cooking time: 12 minutes
Makes: 14

1 stick unsalted butter, just softened
⅓ cup (firmly packed) soft brown sugar
1 egg, at room temperature
1 teaspoon vanilla extract
1⅓ cups all-purpose flour
1 tablespoon unsweetened cocoa powder
1 teaspoon baking powder
½ teaspoon baking soda
⅓ cup milk
heaping ½ cup chopped dark chocolate, melted, cooled
2 cups whipping cream
1½ tablespoons cherry brandy or brandy
1 cup canned pitted cherries, drained, halved
dark chocolate, shaved (using a vegetable peeler),
   to decorate

> **TIP:** Keep unfilled whoopies in an airtight container at room temperature for up to 2 days. They are best filled and decorated just before serving.

1 Preheat the oven to 350°F. Line three large baking sheets with baking paper.
2 Use an electric mixer to beat the butter and sugar in a medium bowl, scraping down the side as necessary, until pale and creamy. Add the egg and vanilla and beat well.
3 Sift the flour, cocoa, baking powder, and baking soda together. With the mixer on low speed, add the flour mixture and milk alternately in two separate batches each. Beat on low speed for 2 minutes or until well combined. Fold through the cooled chocolate.
4 Use a ¾ inch plain nozzle to pipe 28 x 1¾ inch rounds of the mixture onto the baking sheets, leaving 2 inches between them to allow for spreading. Bake for 12 minutes, swapping the baking sheets around after 8 minutes, or until just firm to the touch. Allow to cool for 2 minutes on the baking sheets then transfer to a cake rack to cool completely.
5 Whisk the cream until firm peaks form. Brush the flat sides of half the whoopies with the brandy. Use a ⅝ inch star nozzle to pipe the whipped cream onto the brandy sides, then top with the cherry halves. Sandwich with the remaining whoopies, pressing lightly. Pipe a rosette of the remaining whipped cream on top of each whoopie then decorate with the chocolate shavings.

Rum & raisin whoopies

Preparation time: 25 minutes (+ cooling time)
Cooking time: 15 minutes
Makes: 16

½ cup dark raisins (see tip)
2 tablespoons dark rum
1 stick unsalted butter, just softened
½ cup (firmly packed) soft brown sugar
1 egg, at room temperature
1 teaspoon vanilla extract
1¼ cups all-purpose flour
1 teaspoon baking powder
½ teaspoon baking soda
½ cup milk
1 quantity vanilla glaze (see page 120), made with
2 teaspoons dark rum instead of 1 tablespoon
of the boiling water

TIP: Golden raisins can be used in place of the dark raisins if you like.

Keep unfilled whoopies in an airtight container at room temperature for up to 2 days. They are best filled and iced just before serving.

1 Place the raisins and rum in a small saucepan over medium heat until the rum is almost simmering. Remove from the heat and set aside to cool completely.
2 Preheat the oven to 350°F. Line three large baking sheets with baking paper.
3 Use an electric mixer to beat the butter and sugar in a medium bowl, scraping down the side as necessary, until pale and creamy. Add the egg and vanilla and beat well.
4 Sift the flour, baking powder, and baking soda together. With the mixer on low speed, add the flour mixture and milk alternately in two separate batches each. Beat on low speed for 2 minutes or until well combined. Drain the raisins and discard any liquid. Fold the raisins through the mixture.

5 Spoon 32 heaping tablespoonfuls of the mixture onto the baking sheets, leaving 2 inches between them to allow for spreading. Bake for 12 minutes, swapping the baking sheets around after 8 minutes, or until light golden and just firm to the touch. Allow to cool for 2 minutes on the baking sheets then transfer to a cake rack to cool completely.
6 Spread the glaze onto the flat sides of half the whoopies. Sandwich with the remaining whoopies. Drizzle the remaining glaze over the top of each whoopie (you may need to add more boiling water to thin it slightly). Allow to stand until set.

Praline whoopies

Preparation time: 40 minutes
Cooking time: 30 minutes
Makes: 8

⅓ cup unsalted butter, just softened
⅓ cup superfine sugar
1 egg, at room temperature
1 teaspoon vanilla extract
1 cup all-purpose flour
½ teaspoon baking powder
½ teaspoon baking soda
¼ cup milk
1¼ cups whipping cream

Praline
⅓ cup slivered almonds, toasted
⅓ cup pistachio nuts, toasted
1 cup superfine sugar

TIP: Keep the praline in an airtight container at room temperature for up to 1 day. The extra crushed praline can be used to decorate desserts or for sprinkling on ice cream.

Keep unfilled whoopies in an airtight container at room temperature for up to 2 days. They are best filled just before serving.

1 Preheat the oven to 350°F. Line three large and one small baking sheets with baking paper.
2 For the praline, spread the nuts on the small baking sheet. Stir the sugar and ⅓ cup water in a medium saucepan over low heat until the sugar dissolves, then bring to a boil. Simmer, without stirring, for 10–15 minutes or until golden. Pour toffee over nuts. Stand until set, then break into pieces. Process the praline in a food processor using the pulse button until coarsely crushed. Remove half the praline and reserve. Process the remaining praline until finely crushed.
3 Use an electric mixer to beat the butter and sugar in a medium bowl, scraping down the side as necessary, until pale and creamy. Add the egg and vanilla and beat well.
4 Sift the flour, baking powder, and baking soda together. With the mixer on low speed, add the flour mixture and milk alternately in two separate batches each. Beat on low speed for 2 minutes or until well combined. Stir though ⅓ cup of the finely crushed praline.
5 Use a ¾ inch plain nozzle to pipe 16 x 2½ inch rounds of the mixture onto the large baking sheets, leaving 2 inches between them. Bake for 10–12 minutes, swapping the baking sheets around halfway through cooking, or until light golden and just firm to the touch. Cool for 2 minutes on the baking sheets; transfer to a cake rack to cool completely.
6 Whisk the cream until firm peaks form. Use a ¾ inch plain nozzle to pipe the cream onto the flat sides of half the whoopies, spreading to the edges. Sandwich with the remaining whoopies. Roll the sides of the whoopies in the reserved praline to coat.

Opera whoopies

Preparation time: 30 minutes
Cooking time: 10 minutes
Makes: 12

1 stick unsalted butter, just softened
¾ cup superfine sugar
1 egg, at room temperature
1 teaspoon vanilla extract
1⅔ cups all-purpose flour,
   plus 2 tablespoons extra
1½ teaspoons baking powder
½ teaspoon baking soda
½ cup ground almonds
⅓ cup milk, or just enough to make a very thick batter
2 tablespoons unsweetened cocoa powder, sifted
1 cup chopped dark chocolate, melted
1 quantity vanilla buttercream (see page 118),
   made with 1 tablespoon Baileys Irish Cream

> **TIP:** Keep filled whoopies in an airtight container in the fridge for up to 3 days. Stand at room temperature for 30 minutes before serving.

1 Preheat the oven to 350°F. Line three large baking sheets with baking paper.

2 Use an electric mixer to beat the butter and sugar in a medium bowl, scraping down the side as necessary, until pale and creamy. Add the egg and vanilla and beat well.

3 Sift the flour, baking powder, and baking soda together. With the mixer on low speed, add the flour mixture, ground almonds, and milk alternately in two separate batches each. Beat on low speed until just combined.

4 Transfer half the mixture to a clean bowl, add the extra flour, and mix with a wooden spoon until just combined. Add the cocoa to the remaining mixture and mix until combined.

5 Use a ½ inch nozzle to pipe 12 x 2 inch rounds of the vanilla mixture onto the baking sheets, leaving 2 inches between them to allow for spreading. Repeat with the cocoa mixture to make another 12 rounds. Bake for 8–10 minutes or until light golden and just firm to the touch. Allow to cool for 2 minutes on the baking sheets then transfer to a cake rack to cool completely.

6 Spread the melted chocolate onto the flat sides of the vanilla whoopies. Spread or pipe the buttercream onto the flat sides of the chocolate whoopies. Sandwich the whoopies together.

Chocolate mud whoopies

Preparation time: 35 minutes
Cooking time: 12 minutes
Makes: 18

1 tablespoon instant coffee granules
1 stick unsalted butter, just softened
¾ cup (lightly packed) soft brown sugar
1 egg, at room temperature
1 teaspoon vanilla extract
heaping ¾ cup dark chocolate, melted, cooled
1½ cups all-purpose flour
⅔ cup unsweetened cocoa powder
2 teaspoons baking powder
½ teaspoon baking soda
⅓ cup milk
1 quantity dark chocolate ganache (see page 122)
⅓ cup chopped or shaved dark chocolate
    (using a vegetable peeler), to decorate

TIP: Keep filled (but not decorated) whoopies in an airtight container in the fridge for up to 3 days. Stand at room temperature for 30 minutes and decorate just before serving.

1 Preheat the oven to 315°F. Line three large baking sheets with baking paper. Combine the coffee granules with 1 tablespoon boiling water. Set aside to cool.

2 Use an electric mixer to beat the butter and sugar in a medium bowl, scraping down the side as necessary, until pale and creamy. Add the egg and vanilla and beat well. Add the cooled chocolate and mix on low speed until just combined.

3 Sift the flour, cocoa, baking powder, and baking soda together. With the mixer on low speed, add the flour mixture and milk alternately in two separate batches each. Add the cooled coffee mixture and beat on low speed until just combined.

4 Use wet hands to roll 36 tablespoonfuls of the mixture into balls. (If the mixture is too soft, refrigerate until firm enough to roll.) Place the balls on the baking sheets, leaving 2 inches between them to allow for spreading. Bake for 10–12 minutes, swapping the baking sheets around after 8 minutes, or until just firm to the touch. Allow to cool for 2 minutes on the baking sheets then transfer to a cake rack to cool completely.

5 Spoon or pipe the chocolate ganache onto the flat sides of half the whoopies. Sandwich with the remaining whoopies. Use a ½ inch star nozzle to pipe a rosette, using the remaining ganache, on top of each whoopie then sprinkle with the chocolate.

Orange almond whoopies with strawberries & mascarpone

Preparation time: 35 minutes
Cooking time: 12 minutes
Makes: 12

2 oranges
1 stick unsalted butter, just softened
¾ cup superfine sugar
1 egg, at room temperature
1 teaspoon vanilla extract
1¾ cups all-purpose flour
1 teaspoon baking powder
½ teaspoon baking soda
1 cup ground almonds
confectioners' sugar, to dust

Filling
1½ cups mascarpone cheese
½ cup confectioners' sugar, sifted
2⅔ cups thinly sliced strawberries

TIP: Keep unfilled whoopies in an airtight container at room temperature for up to 2 days. They are best filled just before serving.

1 Preheat the oven to 350°F. Line three large baking sheets with baking paper.
2 Finely grate the zest from the oranges and set aside. Juice the oranges and measure out 1 cup plus 1 tablespoon. Use an electric mixer to beat the butter and sugar in a medium bowl, scraping down the side as necessary, until pale and creamy. Add the egg, orange zest, and vanilla and beat well.
3 Sift the flour, baking powder, and baking soda together. Stir in the ground almonds. With the mixer on low speed, add the flour mixture and orange juice alternately in two separate batches. Beat on low speed for 2 minutes or until well combined.

4 Spoon 24 slightly heaping tablespoonfuls of the mixture onto the baking sheets, leaving 2 inches between them to allow for spreading. Bake for 10–12 minutes, swapping the baking sheets around after 7 minutes, or until light golden and just firm to the touch. Allow to cool for 2 minutes on the baking sheets then transfer to a cake rack to cool completely.
5 To make the filling, use a wooden spoon to stir the mascarpone and confectioners' sugar in a bowl until just combined. Arrange the sliced strawberries on the flat sides of half the whoopies. Use a ¾ inch plain nozzle to pipe the filling over the strawberries. Sandwich with the remaining whoopies, pressing together gently. Dust with confectioners' sugar.

Triple chocolate whoopies

Preparation time: 25 minutes
Cooking time: 15 minutes
Makes: 15

1 stick unsalted butter, just softened
2/3 cup (firmly packed) soft brown sugar
1 egg, at room temperature
1 teaspoon vanilla extract
1½ cups all-purpose flour
2/3 cup unsweetened cocoa powder
1½ teaspoons baking powder
½ teaspoon baking soda
2/3 cup milk
1/3 cup chopped dark chocolate
1/3 cup chopped white chocolate
1/3 cup chopped milk chocolate
1 quantity white, dark, or milk chocolate ganache
(see page 122)

> **TIP:** Keep filled whoopies in an airtight container in the fridge for up to 3 days. Stand at room temperature for 30 minutes before serving.

1 Preheat the oven to 350°F. Line three large baking sheets with baking paper.
2 Use an electric mixer to beat the butter and sugar in a medium bowl, scraping down the side as necessary, until pale and creamy. Add the egg and vanilla and beat well.
3 Sift the flour, cocoa, baking powder, and baking soda together. With the mixer on low speed, add the flour mixture and milk alternately in two separate batches each. Beat on low speed until just combined. Fold in all the chocolate.

4 Spoon 30 heaping tablespoonfuls of the mixture onto the baking sheets, leaving 2 inches between them to allow for spreading. Bake for 12–15 minutes, swapping the sheets around after 8 minutes, or until just firm to the touch. (Do not overcook, or they will dry out.) Allow to cool for 2 minutes on the sheets then transfer to a cake rack to cool completely.
5 Spread or pipe the chocolate ganache onto the flat sides of half the whoopies. Sandwich with the remaining whoopies.

Hot toddy whoopies

Preparation time: 50 minutes (+ 2 hours standing time)
Cooking time: 12 minutes
Makes: 10

1 stick unsalted butter, just softened
¾ cup (firmly packed) soft brown sugar
1 egg, at room temperature
1½ teaspoons vanilla extract
1 tablespoon finely grated lemon zest
2 cups all-purpose flour
1 teaspoon baking powder
½ teaspoon baking soda
2 teaspoons ground cinnamon
½ teaspoon freshly grated or ground nutmeg
½ teaspoon ground cloves
⅓ cup milk
¼ cup whisky
½ quantity vanilla glaze (see page 120), made
   with hot whisky instead of the water
1 quantity vanilla buttercream (see page 118),
   made with 1 tablespoon whisky

TIP: Keep unfilled whoopies in an airtight container at room temperature for up to 3 days. They are best filled and iced on the day of serving.

1 Preheat the oven to 350°F. Line three large baking sheets with baking paper.
2 Use an electric mixer to beat the butter and sugar in a medium bowl, scraping down the side as necessary, until pale and creamy. Add the egg, vanilla, and zest and beat well.
3 Sift the flour, baking powder, baking soda and spices together. With the mixer on low speed, add the flour mixture and milk alternately in two separate batches each, then mix in the whisky. Beat on low speed for 2 minutes or until well combined.
4 Spoon 20 even, heaping tablespoonfuls of the mixture onto the baking sheets, leaving 2 inches between them to allow for spreading. Bake for 12 minutes, swapping the baking

sheets around after 8 minutes, or until light golden and just firm to the touch. Allow to cool for 2 minutes on the baking sheets then transfer to a cake rack to cool completely.
5 Coat the tops of half the whoopies with the glaze. Stand for 30 minutes or until firm.
6 Use any remaining glaze to drizzle over the iced whoopies, thinning it with a little more whisky or water, if necessary. Stand iced whoopies for 1½ hours or until the glaze is completely set.
7 Use a ⅝ inch star nozzle to pipe the buttercream onto the flat sides of the un-iced whoopies. Sandwich with the iced whoopies (take care to not crack the glaze).

Chocolate, orange, & ricotta whoopies

Preparation time: 30 minutes
Cooking time: 10 minutes
Makes: 13

1 stick unsalted butter, just softened
⅓ cup (firmly packed) soft brown sugar
1 egg, at room temperature
1 teaspoon vanilla extract
1⅓ cups all-purpose flour
½ teaspoon baking powder
½ teaspoon baking soda
1 tablespoon unsweetened cocoa powder,
  plus extra, to dust
⅓ cup milk
heaping ½ cup chopped dark chocolate, melted, cooled
candied orange zest (see page 122) (optional), to decorate

Orange ricotta filling
1¼ cups firm, fresh ricotta cheese
2 teaspoons finely grated orange zest
1 teaspoon vanilla extract
½ cup confectioners' sugar, sifted

> **TIP:** Keep unfilled whoopies in an airtight container at room temperature for up to 2 days. They are best filled and decorated just before serving.

1 Preheat the oven to 350°F. Line three large baking sheets with baking paper.
2 Use an electric mixer to beat the butter and sugar in a medium bowl, scraping down the side as necessary, until pale and creamy. Add the egg and vanilla and beat well.
3 Sift the flour, baking powder, baking soda, and cocoa together. With the mixer on low speed, add the flour mixture and milk alternately in two separate batches each. Add the cooled chocolate. Beat on low speed for 2 minutes or until well combined.
4 Use a ¾ inch plain nozzle to pipe 26 x 1¾ inch rounds of the mixture onto the baking sheets, leaving 2 inches between them. Bake for

10 minutes, swapping the baking sheets around after 8 minutes, or until light golden and just firm to the touch. Cool for 2 minutes on the baking sheets then transfer to a cake rack to cool completely.
5 To make the orange ricotta filling, use an electric mixer to beat the ricotta, zest, and vanilla in a small bowl until smooth. Gradually beat in the confectioners' sugar.
6 Use a ½ inch plain nozzle to pipe the filling onto the flat sides of half the whoopies. Sandwich with the remaining whoopies. Dust with cocoa and top with the candied orange zest to decorate, if using.

Whoopies
big & small

Petit four whoopies

Preparation time: 1½ hours (+ 2 hours setting time)
Cooking time: 8 minutes
Makes: 48

1 stick unsalted butter, just softened
¾ cup superfine sugar
1 egg, at room temperature
1 teaspoon vanilla extract
1¾ cups all-purpose flour
1 teaspoon baking powder
½ teaspoon baking soda
1 cup ground almonds
½ cup milk
1 quantity vanilla glaze (see page 120)
3 food colorings of your choice
2 quantities vanilla buttercream (see page 118)
48 edible small sugar flowers, to decorate

TIP: Keep unfilled and un-iced whoopies in an airtight container at room temperature for up to 3 days. They are best filled and iced on the day of serving.

1 Preheat the oven to 350°F. Line three large baking sheets with baking paper.
2 Use an electric mixer to beat the butter and sugar in a medium bowl, scraping down the side as necessary, until pale and creamy. Add the egg and vanilla and beat well.
3 Sift the flour, baking powder, and baking soda together. Stir in the ground almonds. With the mixer on low speed, add the flour mixture and milk alternately in two separate batches each. Beat on low speed for 2 minutes or until well combined.
4 Use a ½ inch nozzle to pipe 96 x ¾ inch rounds of the mixture onto the baking sheets, leaving 1¼ inch between them to allow for spreading. Bake for 8 minutes, swapping the baking sheets around after 5 minutes, or until

light golden and firm to the touch. Allow to cool for 2 minutes on the baking sheets then transfer to a cake rack to cool completely.
5 Divide the glaze into equal portions in three separate bowls. Add enough food coloring to each to tint to the desired color. Use a flat-bladed or palette knife to coat the tops of half the whoopies with the glaze then set aside on a cake rack for 2 hours or until set.
6 Use a ½ inch star or plain nozzle to pipe the vanilla buttercream onto the flat sides of the remaining whoopies. Sandwich with the iced whoopies, pressing gently to join (take care to not crack the glaze). Pipe a very small amount of the remaining buttercream on top of each whoopie and decorate with a sugar flower.

Mini florentine whoopies

Preparation time: 25 minutes (+ cooling time)
Cooking time: 40 minutes
Makes: 50

scant ⅔ cup butter, chopped
½ cup honey
2 cups mixed dried fruit
1 cup slivered almonds
⅔ cup candied cherries, chopped
½ cup all-purpose flour
½ teaspoon baking powder
1 egg, lightly whisked
1 tablespoon finely grated orange zest
1 quantity dark chocolate ganache
   (see page 122)

1 Preheat the oven to 350°F. Line two large baking sheets with baking paper.
2 Place the butter and honey in a small saucepan over medium heat and stir until the butter melts. Remove from the heat and cool to room temperature.
3 Combine the mixed fruit, almonds, and candied cherries in a large bowl. Sift over the flour and baking powder and stir until well combined.
4 Add the butter mixture, egg, and orange zest to the fruit and stir until well combined.
5 Spoon 40 heaping teaspoonfuls of the mixture onto the baking sheets, leaving 1¼ inches between them to allow for spreading. Use the back of a teaspoon to press down gently to flatten the mixture and form 1½ inch rounds. Bake for 12 minutes, swapping the baking sheets around after 7 minutes, or until golden and firm to the touch. Allow to cool completely on the baking sheets. Repeat with the remaining mixture to make 60 more whoopie rounds.
6 Spread the chocolate ganache onto the flat sides of half the whoopies. Sandwich with the remaining whoopies.

TIP: Keep filled whoopies in an airtight container in the fridge for up to 1 week. Serve at room temperature. These whoopies are unsuitable to freeze.

Christmas whoopies

Preparation time: 25 minutes (+ 6 hours macerating time)
Cooking time: 15 minutes
Makes: seven 3½ inch square whoopies

2 cups mixed dried fruit
½ cup candied cherries, halved
¼ cup dark rum
1 stick unsalted butter, just softened
¼ cup honey
⅓ cup (firmly packed) dark brown sugar
1 egg, at room temperature
1 teaspoon vanilla extract
2 cups all-purpose flour
1 teaspoon baking powder
½ teaspoon baking soda
1 teaspoon mixed spice
1 teaspoon ground cinnamon
⅓ cup milk
1 tablespoon finely grated orange zest
⅔ quantity marshmallow frosting (see page 123)
confectioners' sugar, to dust

TIP: Keep unfilled whoopies in an airtight container at room temperature for up to 3 days. They are best filled on the day of serving.

1 Place the mixed fruit, candied cherries, and rum in a bowl. Cover and allow to macerate at room temperature for 6 hours or overnight.
2 Preheat the oven to 325°F. Line three large baking sheets with baking paper. Mark 14 x 3¼ inch squares on the baking paper, leaving 2 inches between them to allow for spreading, then turn the paper over.
3 Use an electric mixer to beat the butter, honey, and sugar in a medium bowl, scraping down the side as necessary, until pale and creamy. Add the egg and vanilla and beat well.
4 Sift the flour, baking powder, baking soda, and spices together. With the mixer on low speed, add the flour mixture and milk alternately in two separate batches each. Beat on low

speed until just combined. Fold in the mixed fruit and orange zest.
5 Divide the mixture among the squares, using the squares marked as a guide. Use the back of a spoon to carefully push the mixture out to the corners. Bake for 15 minutes, swapping the baking sheets around after 9 minutes, or until light golden and just firm to the touch. Allow to cool for 2 minutes on the baking sheets then transfer to a cake rack to cool completely.
6 Spread the warm marshmallow frosting onto the flat sides of half the whoopies. Sandwich with the remaining whoopies. Dust with confectioners' sugar. Cut into quarters to serve.

Mini blueberry & white chocolate whoopies

Preparation time: 25 minutes (+ 20–30 minutes chilling time)
Cooking time: 10 minutes
Makes: 30

1 stick unsalted butter, just softened
¾ cup superfine sugar
1 egg, at room temperature
1 teaspoon vanilla extract
2 cups all-purpose flour
1 teaspoon baking powder
½ teaspoon baking soda
⅔ cup milk
heaping ¾ cup chopped white chocolate, melted,
    cooled to room temperature
1 quantity cream cheese frosting (see page 121)

Sugared blueberries
¼ cup superfine sugar
¾ cup small fresh blueberries
1 egg white, at room temperature, lightly whisked

> **TIP:** Keep filled whoopies (but not decorated with the sugared blueberries) in an airtight container in the fridge for up to 2 days. Allow to stand at room temperature for 30 minutes and decorate with the sugared blueberries before serving.

1 Preheat the oven to 350°F. Line three large baking sheets with baking paper.

2 Use an electric mixer to beat the butter and superfine sugar in a medium bowl, scraping down the side as necessary, until pale and creamy. Add the egg and vanilla and beat well.

3 Sift the flour, baking powder, and baking soda together. With the mixer on low speed, add the flour mixture and milk alternately in two separate batches each. Beat on low speed for 2 minutes or until well combined.

4 Spoon 60 even teaspoonfuls of the mixture onto the baking sheets, leaving 1¼ inches between them to allow for spreading. Bake for 8–10 minutes, swapping the baking sheets around after 6 minutes, or until light golden and just firm to the touch.

Allow to cool for 2 minutes on the baking sheets then transfer to a cake rack to cool completely.

5 Meanwhile, use an electric mixer to beat the cooled chocolate through the cream cheese frosting. Refrigerate for 20–30 minutes or until firm.

6 Use a ⅝ inch plain nozzle to pipe the cream cheese frosting onto the flat sides of half the whoopies, reserving a little of the frosting. Sandwich with the remaining whoopies.

7 To make the sugared blueberries, place the sugar on a small plate. Dip the blueberries into the egg white, drain excess, then roll in the sugar to coat. Set aside to dry on a cake rack. Pipe a small amount of reserved frosting onto the top of each whoopie. Decorate each with two sugared blueberries.

Celebration whoopie cake

Preparation time: 30 minutes
Cooking time: 18 minutes
Serves: 8–10 (makes 1 large whoopie)

1 stick unsalted butter, just softened
½ cup (firmly packed) soft brown sugar
1 egg, at room temperature
1 teaspoon vanilla extract
1¼ cups all-purpose flour
¼ cup unsweetened cocoa powder
½ teaspoon baking powder
½ teaspoon baking soda
½ cup milk
¾ quantity dark chocolate ganache
(see page 122), well chilled
½ quantity chocolate glaze (see page 120)

TIP: Keep unfilled and un-iced whoopie halves in an airtight container at room temperature for up to 2 days. This cake is best filled and iced on the day of serving.

1 Preheat the oven to 350°F. Line two large baking sheets with baking paper. Mark a 7 inch circle on each piece of paper then turn the paper over.

2 Use an electric mixer to beat the butter and sugar in a medium bowl, scraping down the side as necessary, until pale and creamy. Add the egg and vanilla and beat well.

3 Sift the flour, cocoa, baking powder, and baking soda together. With the mixer on low speed, add the flour mixture and milk alternately in two separate batches each. Beat on low speed for 2 minutes or until well combined.

4 Spoon half the mixture into each round, using the marked circles as a guide, then smooth the surface. Bake for 16–18 minutes, swapping the baking sheets around after 10 minutes, or until firm to the touch. Allow to cool for 10 minutes on baking sheets then transfer to a cake rack (top sides up) to cool completely.

5 Use an electric mixer to beat the chilled chocolate ganache in a small bowl for 1 minute or until thickened slightly and paler in color. Place one whoopie, flat side up, on a serving plate. Spread with the ganache. Top with the remaining whoopie, pressing down gently. Drizzle the whoopie with the glaze, allowing it to drizzle down the sides. Decorate with candles, if desired. Serve cut into wedges.

Mini sugar & spice whoopies

Preparation time: 25 minutes
Cooking time: 10 minutes
Makes: 30

1 stick unsalted butter, just softened
1 cup superfine sugar
1 egg, at room temperature
1 teaspoon vanilla extract
2 cups all-purpose flour
1 teaspoon baking powder
½ teaspoon baking soda
3 teaspoons ground cinnamon
1 teaspoon ground ginger
1 teaspoon ground nutmeg
¼ teaspoon ground cloves
⅔ cup milk
1 quantity cream cheese frosting (see page 121)

TIP: Keep filled whoopies in an airtight container in the fridge for up to 3 days. Allow to stand at room temperature for 30 minutes before serving.

1 Preheat the oven to 350°F. Line three large baking sheets with baking paper.
2 Use an electric mixer to beat the butter and ¾ cup of the sugar in a medium bowl, scraping down the side as necessary, until pale and creamy. Add the egg and vanilla and beat well.
3 Sift the flour, baking powder, baking soda, 2 teaspoons of the cinnamon, and the ginger, nutmeg, and cloves together. With the mixer on low speed, add the flour mixture and milk alternately in two separate batches each. Beat on low speed for 2 minutes or until well combined.
4 Use a ½ inch plain nozzle to pipe 60 x 1¼ inch rounds of the mixture onto the baking sheets, leaving 1¼ inches between them to allow for spreading. Bake for 7–10 minutes, swapping the baking sheets around after 5 minutes, or until light golden and just firm to the touch. Allow to cool for 2 minutes on the baking sheets then transfer to a cake rack to cool completely.
5 Use a ½ inch star nozzle to pipe the cream cheese frosting onto the flat sides of half the whoopies. Sandwich with the remaining whoopies.
6 Combine the remaining sugar and cinnamon in a small bowl. Sprinkle the whoopies with the cinnamon sugar.

Small flower whoopies

Preparation time: 40 minutes
Cooking time: 10 minutes
Makes: 15

1 stick unsalted butter, just softened
¾ cup superfine sugar
1 egg, at room temperature
1 teaspoon vanilla extract
2 cups all-purpose flour
1 teaspoon baking powder
½ teaspoon baking soda
⅔ cup milk
1 quantity vanilla buttercream (see page 118),
   made with 2 teaspoons finely grated orange zest
   and 1 teaspoon orange extract (see tip)
9 ounces store-bought ready-made white fondant icing
pink, yellow, green, and/or blue food coloring
edible small sugar flowers, to decorate

> **TIP:** Orange extract is available from supermarkets in the baking aisle.
>
> Keep unfilled whoopies in an airtight container at room temperature for up to 2 days. They are best filled, iced and decorated on the day of serving.

1 Preheat the oven to 350°F. Line three large baking sheets with baking paper.

2 Use an electric mixer to beat the butter and sugar in a medium bowl, scraping down the side as necessary, until pale and creamy. Add the egg and vanilla and beat well.

3 Sift the flour, baking powder, and baking soda together. With the mixer on low speed, add the flour mixture and milk alternately in two separate batches each. Beat on low speed for 2 minutes or until well combined.

4 Spoon 30 even, heaping teaspoonfuls of the mixture onto the baking sheets, leaving 1¼ inches between them to allow for spreading. Bake for 8–10 minutes, swapping baking sheets after 6 minutes, or until light golden and just firm to the touch. Allow to cool for 2 minutes on the baking sheets then transfer to a cake rack to cool completely.

5 Spread or pipe the vanilla buttercream onto the flat sides of half the whoopies. Sandwich with the remaining whoopies.

6 Divide the ready-made fondant into equal portions (depending on the number of colors you want). Flatten each portion and add 2–3 drops of food coloring to each, or enough to tint to the desired color. Fold in to enclose the color and knead gently until tinted evenly. Wrap the fondant portions in plastic wrap. Roll out the fondant portions, one at a time, on a surface lightly dusted with confectioners' sugar to ⅛ inch thick. Use fluted or flower-shaped cutters to cut out the fondant. Brush the underside of the fondant shapes with a little water and place on the tops of the whoopies, pressing gently. Dab the underside of each sugar flower with a little water and press firmly into the top of the fondant to decorate.

Giant choc–coconut whoopie

Preparation time: 35 minutes (+ setting time)
Cooking time: 16 minutes
Serves: 8–10 (makes 1 large whoopie)

1 stick unsalted butter, just softened
¾ cup superfine sugar
1 egg, at room temperature
1 teaspoon vanilla extract
2 cups all-purpose flour
1 teaspoon baking powder
½ teaspoon baking soda
⅔ cup milk
1 quantity chocolate glaze (see page 120),
  made with pure confectioners' sugar
⅔ cup shredded coconut
1 cup whipping cream
½ cup strawberry jam

TIP: Keep unfilled and un-iced whoopie halves in an airtight container at room temperature for up to 2 days. This is best filled, iced and decorated just before serving.

1 Preheat the oven to 350°F. Line two large baking sheets with baking paper. Mark an 8 inch circle on each piece of baking paper then turn the paper over.

2 Use an electric mixer to beat the butter and sugar in a medium bowl, scraping down the side as necessary, until pale and creamy. Add the egg and vanilla and beat well.

3 Sift the flour, baking powder, and baking soda together. With the mixer on low speed, add the flour mixture and milk alternately in two separate batches each. Beat on low speed for 2 minutes or until well combined.

4 Spoon half the mixture into each round, using the marked circles as a guide, then smooth the surface. Bake for 16 minutes,

swapping the baking sheets around after 10 minutes, or until light golden and just firm to the touch. Cool for 10 minutes on the baking sheets then transfer to a cake rack (top sides up) to cool completely.

5 Stand the racks with the cakes on them over the baking sheets and spread the glaze over the cakes, allowing it to drizzle down the sides. Sprinkle both cakes evenly with the coconut. Set aside until the glaze is completely set.

6 To serve, whisk the cream until firm peaks form. Place one whoopie, flat side up, on a serving plate. Spread with the jam and then the cream. Top with the remaining whoopie. Serve cut into wedges.

Basics

Vanilla buttercream

Preparation time: 10 minutes
Makes: enough to generously fill twelve 2¾–3¼ inch whoopies

> scant ¾ cup unsalted butter, just softened
> 1½ teaspoons vanilla extract
> 2 cups confectioners' sugar, sifted

1 Use an electric mixer to beat the butter and vanilla on medium speed for 2 minutes or until smooth and pale.
2 Reduce the speed to low and add the confectioners' sugar, ½ cup at a time, beating well after each addition.

TIP: Keep vanilla buttercream in an airtight container in the fridge for up to 3 days. Bring to room temperature before using.

Chocolate buttercream

Preparation time: 10 minutes
Makes: enough to generously fill twelve 2¾–3¼ inch whoopies

> 1 stick unsalted butter, just softened
> 1 teaspoon vanilla extract
> heaping ½ cup chopped dark chocolate, melted, cooled
> 2 cups confectioners' sugar
> 2½ tablespoons unsweetened cocoa powder
> 1 tablespoon milk

1 Use an electric mixer to beat the butter and vanilla on medium speed for about 2 minutes or until smooth and pale. Add the cooled chocolate and beat until well combined.
2 Sift together the confectioners' sugar and cocoa. With the mixer on low speed, add the confectioners' sugar mixture, ½ cup at a time, alternating with a little of the milk and beating well between additions, until all the confectioners' sugar, cocoa, and milk are incorporated.

TIP: Keep chocolate buttercream in an airtight container in the fridge for up to 3 days. Bring to room temperature before using.

Meringue frosting

Preparation time: 15 minutes
Cooking time: 5 minutes
Makes: enough to generously fill
  twelve 2¾–3¼ inch whoopies

¾ cup superfine sugar
3 egg whites, at room temperature
1⅓ cups unsalted butter, just softened
1½ teaspoons vanilla extract

1 Half-fill a medium saucepan with water. Bring to a simmer over medium heat.
2 Combine the sugar and egg whites in a heatproof bowl large enough to sit snugly into the saucepan without touching the water. Place the bowl over the simmering water and use a balloon whisk to whisk for 4–5 minutes or until the sugar dissolves and the mixture is hot.
3 Transfer the mixture to the bowl of an electric mixer fitted with the whisk attachment and whisk on medium–high speed for about 8 minutes or until a stiff, glossy meringue forms and the mixture cools to room temperature.
4 Reduce the speed to medium then whisk in the butter, a little at a time, until the butter is incorporated and the mixture is smooth. Whisk in the vanilla.
5 Beat the frosting with a wooden spoon or a beater attachment for 1–2 minutes to expel any air pockets.

TIP: Keep meringue frosting in an airtight container in the fridge for up to 3 days. Bring to room temperature before using.

PIPING WHOOPIES: To pipe your whoopies into the correct size, use a round cutter of the specified diameter to trace circles on the baking paper, leaving room between them to allow for spreading. Turn the baking paper over on the baking sheets then pipe the mixture into the marked circles.

FREEZING WHOOPIES: Unless otherwise specified, all unfilled whoopies in this book can be frozen for up to 1 month. Place them in an airtight container, separate any layers with baking paper, and freeze.

Vanilla glaze

Preparation time: 5 minutes
Makes: 1 cup

> 3¼ cups confectioners' sugar, sifted
> ¼ cup boiling water, approximately
> 1 teaspoon vanilla extract

Place the confectioners' sugar in a large heatproof bowl. Use a whisk to slowly stir in the boiling water until the mixture is smooth and has a light coating consistency. Stir in the vanilla. Add a little more water, if necessary, to reach the desired consistency.

TIP: This glaze will thicken on standing so it may be necessary to thin it with a little boiling water if not using it immediately.

Keep vanilla glaze, with the surface directly covered with plastic wrap to prevent a crust forming, at room temperature for up to 1 day.

Chocolate glaze

Preparation time: 5 minutes
Makes: 1 cup

> 3½ cups confectioners' sugar
> ¼ cup unsweetened cocoa powder
> ¼ cup boiling water, approximately
> 1 teaspoon vanilla extract

Sift together the confectioners' sugar and cocoa into a large bowl. Use a whisk to slowly stir in the boiling water until the mixture is smooth and has a light coating consistency. Stir in the vanilla. Add a little more water, if necessary, to reach the desired consistency.

TIP: This glaze will thicken on standing so it may be necessary to thin it with a little boiling water if not using it immediately.

Keep chocolate glaze, with the surface directly covered with plastic wrap to prevent a crust forming, at room temperature for up to 1 day.

Royal icing

Preparation time: 10 minutes
Makes: about 1½ cups

> 2 egg whites
> 1½ teaspoons lemon juice
> 2 cups pure confectioners' sugar, sifted
> food coloring, as needed

1 Combine the egg whites and 1 teaspoon of the lemon juice in a small bowl. Use an electric mixer fitted with the whisk attachment to whisk until foamy.
2 With the motor running, add the confectioners' sugar, ½ cup at a time, whisking well after each addition. Continue whisking until the mixture is thick, white, and glossy. Add the remaining lemon juice and whisk to combine.

TIP: Use royal icing to pipe names, numbers, letters, or other decorations, or to stick cachous or other decorations, on the tops of your whoopies.

Keep royal icing in an airtight container, with the surface directly covered with plastic wrap, at room temperature for up to 1 day. Thin the icing with a little boiling water to reach the desired consistency, if necessary.

Cream cheese frosting

Preparation time: 10 minutes
Makes: enough to generously fill twelve 2¾–3¼ inch whoopies

> scant ⅔ cup cream cheese, just softened, chopped
> ⅓ cup unsalted butter, just softened
> 1½ cups confectioners' sugar, sifted
> 1 teaspoon vanilla extract

1 Use an electric mixer to beat the cream cheese and butter on medium speed until smooth and well combined.
2 Reduce the speed to low and add the confectioners' sugar, ½ cup at a time, beating well after each addition. Add the vanilla and beat until combined.

TIP: Keep cream cheese frosting in an airtight container in the fridge for up to 3 days. Bring to room temperature before using.

Dark chocolate ganache

Preparation time: 5 minutes (+ 30–60 minutes chilling time)
Makes: enough to generously fill twelve 2¾–3¼ inch whoopies

> 9 ounces dark chocolate, chopped
> ¾ cup whipping cream

1 Place the chocolate in a large heatproof bowl and set aside.
2 Heat the cream in a small saucepan over medium heat until almost simmering. Pour over the chocolate and set aside for 2–3 minutes. Stir until the chocolate melts and the mixture is well combined.
3 Refrigerate for 30–60 minutes, stirring often, or until thickened to a thick, spreadable consistency.

TIP: Be sure to use good-quality chocolate. When working with white chocolate, do not allow it to get too hot. Make sure you chill the ganache thoroughly if whisking before using.

Keep ganache in an airtight container in the fridge for up to 4 days. You may have to stand it at room temperature to soften slightly before spreading or piping.

Variations

Milk chocolate ganache: Replace the dark chocolate with milk chocolate.
White chocolate ganache: Replace the dark chocolate with white chocolate.

CANDIED ORANGE ZEST: Place 2 tablespoons orange zest strips (use a zester) in a small saucepan. Add ¼ cup water, or to cover, and bring to a boil. Drain and repeat. Drain well. Combine ½ cup sugar and 2 tablespoons water in the same pan. Stir over low heat until the sugar dissolves. Add the zest. Simmer for 10 minutes, stirring with a fork to separate the strands, or until translucent and tender. Drain and spread the zest on a cake rack. Set aside for 30 minutes or until dry.

Marshmallow frosting

Preparation time: 15 minutes
Cooking time: 12 minutes
Makes: enough to generously fill twelve 2¾–3¼ inch whoopies

>   1 tablespoon liquid glucose
>   ⅓ cup boiling water
>   1½ cups superfine sugar
>   2 egg whites, at room temperature
>   1 teaspoon vanilla extract
>   ¼ teaspoon cream of tartar
>   1½ cups white marshmallows, chopped

1 Half-fill a large saucepan with water. Bring to a simmer over medium heat.
2 Place the glucose and boiling water in a heatproof bowl large enough to sit snugly into the saucepan without touching the water. Allow to stand until the glucose softens. Stir to combine well. Add the sugar, egg whites, vanilla, and cream of tartar, and use a balloon whisk to whisk until well combined.
3 With the bowl over the simmering water, use a handheld electric mixer to beat the mixture for about 8 minutes or until it is very thick, white, and glossy. Add the marshmallows and continue beating for 3 minutes or until the marshmallows melt and the mixture is smooth and thick.
4 Remove the bowl from the saucepan and continue beating for 3–4 minutes or until the mixture is slightly cooled. Add any optional flavors or colors and whisk to mix well.

TIP: Use marshmallow frosting while it is still warm as it will set when cooled. It is unsuitable to make in advance.

From left: vanilla buttercream, colored vanilla glaze, and dark chocolate ganache

Index

METRO BOOKS
New York

An Imprint of Sterling Publishing
387 Park Avenue South
New York, NY 10016

METRO BOOKS and the distinctive Metro Books logo are trademarks of Sterling Publishing Co., Inc.

© 2012 by Murdoch Books Pty Limited
Illustrations © 2012 by Murdoch Books Pty Limited

This 2012 edition published by Metro Books by arrangement with Murdoch Books Pty Limited

ISBN 978-1-4351-3792-9

For information about custom editions, special sales, and premium and corporate purchases, please contact Sterling Special Sales at 800-805-5489 or specialsales@sterlingpublishing.com.

Manufactured in China

2 4 6 8 10 9 7 5 3 1

www.sterlingpublishing.com